**BORGES**

## CONTINUUM *READER'S GUIDES*

Continuum *Reader's Guides* are clear, concise and accessible introductions to classic literary texts. Each book explores the themes, context, criticism and influence of key works, providing a practical introduction to close reading and guiding the reader towards a thorough understanding of the text. Ideal for undergraduate students, the guides provide an essential resource for anyone who needs to get to grips with a literary text.

*Achebe's* Things Fall Apart – Ode Ogede
*Atwood's* The Handmaid's Tale – Gina Wisker
*Austen's* Emma – Gregg A. Hecimovich
*Borges' Short Stories* – Rex Butler
*Bram Stoker's* Dracula – William Hughes
*Chaucer's* The Canterbury Tales – Gail Ashton
*Conrad's* Heart of Darkness – Allan Simmons
*Dickens's* Great Expectations – Ian Brinton
*Eliot's* Middlemarch – Josie Billington
*Fitzgerald's* The Great Gatsby – Nicolas Tredell
*Fowles'* The French Lieutenant's Woman – William Stephenson
*James's* The Turn of the Screw – Leonard Orr
*Joyce's* Ulysses – Sean Sheehan
*Salinger's* The Catcher in the Rye – Sarah Graham
*Shelley's* Frankenstein – Graham Allen
*William Blake's* Poetry – Jonathan Roberts
*Woolf's* To the Lighthouse – Janet Winston

# BORGES' SHORT STORIES

## A Reader's Guide

### REX BUTLER

continuum

**Continuum International Publishing Group**

The Tower Building  80 Maiden Lane
11 York Road  Suite 704
London SE1 7NX  New York, NY 10038

www.continuumbooks.com

© Rex Butler 2010

**British Library Cataloguing-in-Publication Data**
A catalogue record for this book is available from the British Library.

ISBN:  978-0-8264-4298-7 (hardback)
978-0-8264-5213-9 (paperback)

**Library of Congress Cataloging-in-Publication Data**
A catalog record for this book is available from the Library of Congress.

Typeset by Newgen Imaging Systems Pvt Ltd, Chennai, India
Printed and bound in Great Britain by CPI Antony Rowe, Chippenham, Wiltshire

# CONTENTS

# LIST OF QUOTATIONS AND ABBREVIATIONS

The following texts are indicated by initials:

*A*    'An Autobiographical Essay', in *The Aleph and Other Stories 1933–69*, trans. Norman Thomas di Giovanni, Picador, London, 1973.

*OC*    Jorge Luis Borges, *Obras completas* (4 vols.), Emecé, Barcelona, 1989.

*CF*    Jorge Luis Borges, *Collected Fictions*, trans. Andrew Hurley, Penguin Books, New York, 1998.

*SP*    Jorge Luis Borges, *Selected Poems*, Alexander Coleman (ed.), Penguin Books, New York, 2000.

*TL*    Jorge Luis Borges, *The Total Library: Non-Fiction 1922–86*, Eliot Weinberger (ed.), Penguin Books, London, 1999.

Many of the references in the main text will be found in the Annotated Bibliography, which contains the various books and articles relevant to each chapter.

Consistent with the format of the *Reader's Guide* series, a number of Study Questions for students have been appended to the end of each chapter.

# CHAPTER 1

# CONTEXTS

In March 1957, the subject of this book wrote a short text, 'Borges and I', for *La Biblioteca*, the journal of the National Library of Argentina. By this time, he was already well known to a large Argentine audience, and increasingly so overseas through a series of prestigious translations. He could no longer see, and was unable to write the intricately wrought fictions, often involving philosophical problems, for which he had become recognized. This short text 'Borges and I' would subsequently be included in the 1960 collection *El hacedor* (*The Maker*, but translated into English as *Dreamtigers* in 1963). It is in this collection that Borges first reshapes his public persona into that of a blind Homeric bard; a genial, if occasionally distracted, old man who somehow embodies the entire history of literature. 'Borges and I' is a text that at once is part of this refashioning and comments on it. It begins with a warning against the attempt to biographize the writer, to identify the maker of the work of art with the person behind them. In 'Borges and I', these two selves are shown not to be the same. Though maintaining a cordial relationship, they are not simply identical to each other. As Borges writes:

> It's Borges, the other one, that things happen to. I walk through Buenos Aires and I pause – mechanically now, perhaps – to gaze through the arch of an entryway and its inner door; news of Borges reaches me by mail, or I see his name on a list of academics or in some biographical dictionary. My taste runs to hourglasses, maps, eighteenth-century typography, etymologies, the taste of coffee, and the prose of Robert Louis Stevenson; Borges shares those preferences, but in a vain sort of way that turns them into the accoutrements of an actor. (*CF*, 324)

The first comedy here is that Borges literalizes the impersonality required for the work of art: Borges the writer becomes another person with whom the narrator (the flesh-and-blood Borges) can have a relationship. But the deeper comedy lies in the fact that, far from Borges the person controlling Borges the writer, it is the writer who controls the person. This ordinary Borges with his everyday interests and obsession is a creation of the writer Borges, one of the masks he uses to disguise himself. (If there is a Robert Louis Stevenson text that Borges has a preference for, it is surely *Dr Jekyll and Mr Hyde*.) Thus Borges is telling us, exactly at that moment in his career when his work appears to lend itself to an autobiographical explanation, that even this confession is not to be trusted. It is a creation of Borges the writer, whom we also find described in the story and his preferences given. And yet the question must be asked: from where is the writer described? Who sees the relation between Borges the man and Borges the writer? Who is the Borges who writes about 'Borges' as opposed to the 'I'? It is *this* impossible position – and of course the infinite regress it opens up – that we would say is the real 'Borges', the one for whom both the man and the writer are fictions. It is the Borges for whom all biographies are inadequate, and who is not to be identified with anything in his texts either. It is Borges as a pure space or speaking position, and who is only the permanent doubt: 'I am not sure which of us it is that's writing this page' (*CF*, 324).

\* \* \*

The great Argentine writer Jorge Luis Borges was born on 24 August 1899 in downtown Buenos Aires. His family on his mother's side had been Argentine for several generations, and included amongst it several members who were said to have died defending an early version of Argentine democracy against the tyrant Juan Manuel de Rosas. His family on his father's side was in part made up of recent arrivals, with his father's mother coming from Staffordshire with her father, who was to edit Argentina's first English-language newspaper. Borges' mother was said to have permanently resented her family's loss of status and fortune thanks to Rosas, and to have been obsessed with her family's *criollo* (Spanish Argentine) heritage. She was a devoted wife to her husband, looking after him when he was no longer able to work due to a degenerative eye condition, which Borges also was to inherit, and a loving mother to Borges and his younger sister Norah. Borges' father was a far more intellectual and forward-looking figure, who was interested, before he went blind, in literature and ideas. He worked as a lawyer and part-time psychology lecturer, and described himself as a follower of the nineteenth-century English anarchist Herbert Spencer. Borges for much of his life moved between these two conflicting sets of values: the nationalism and nostalgia of his mother and the cosmopolitanism and anti-authoritarianism of his father. Indeed, this split could be seen to correspond to the two languages Borges spoke at home: his mother's Spanish and his father's (through his paternal grandmother's) English. Spanish for Borges was always 'long and cumbersome' (*A*, 135), and he was constantly seeking to move away from it. English, on the other hand, was the language of literature and the world, a language that he often 'wished had been my birthright', but that he felt 'unworthy to handle' (*A*, 165). In fact, Borges frequently described his father's library of English books, which he read voraciously as a young man, as the 'chief event in my life' (*A*, 129); and the provincial and slightly out-of-date taste of his father was indelibly to shape Borges' own literary universe and was, to some extent, the basis of his literary revolution: Kipling, Stevenson, Wells, Shaw, the English translation of Cervantes' *Don Quixote*, Sir Richard Burton's translation of *The Thousand and One Nights* . . .

For much of his early life, Borges stayed at home with his sister, privately educated by an English governess. Both his mother's snobbishness and his father's distaste for such institutions as state education were satisfied by this solution. When Borges did finally go to school at the advanced age of eleven, he was a shy, myopic boy, who was unused to the company of other children and was subsequently bullied. He was soon taken out of class and was not to return to school for several years. It was an unhappy, fragmented introduction to learning that was undoubtedly to lead to Borges' lifelong distrust of pedagogy and all official curricula. In 1914, partly to undergo a series of operations to try to save his sight and partly to give his children a European education, Borges' father took his family off to Europe. Argentina at the time was one of the world's most prosperous countries, riding high on the beef exports that refrigerated shipping had recently made possible, and Europe was comparatively cheap. The family, however, was forced to stay longer than originally intended due to the outbreak of the First World War; and, after visiting London and Paris, Borges was sent to the exclusive and strictly Protestant Collège Calvin in Geneva, where the family settled down for the duration. During his time there, Borges received a rigorous education, learning to read and speak French and Latin, which was part of the school curriculum. It was also around this time, at the relatively precocious age of seventeen, that Borges undertook his first literary steps. He had always been encouraged to write by his father, who had himself unrealized literary ambitions. Indeed, at the tender age of ten, Borges had made a translation of Oscar Wilde's short story 'The Happy Prince', which appeared in the Buenos Aires daily *El país*. In Geneva, he began to read French and German literature seriously and in great quantities: Baudelaire, Rimbaud, Nietzsche Schopenhauer. He became infatuated with the poetry of Walt Whitman, and fell in with a group of adolescents sharing similar tastes and ambitions. This involvement in literature continued when the family moved to Spain in 1919. Here Borges began to participate fully in the adult literary life, getting his first poem published ('Himno del mar' or 'Hymn to the Sea') and joining up with one of the *tertulias* or weekly literary gatherings held in a pub or bar and presided over by a real poet or writer.

Borges carried on this literary activity when the family returned finally to Buenos Aires in March 1921. Somewhat unusually from our perspective, there was no expectation that he would finish his education and go to university – he had not completed his baccalauréat while in Switzerland – or even find a job. His father by this point was unable to work because of his poor eyesight, so the family lived off savings and the income produced by renting their house. Borges engaged himself in an endless whirl of literary activity, agitating on behalf of the avant-garde literary movement that he had brought back with him from Spain. *Ultraísmo* was a word originally coined by the Sevillian poet Rafael Cansinos-Asséns, who spoke in an interview of the necessity for poets to be 'ultra-Romantic'. The movement was notable for its Futurist-like obsession with modern technology and its coining of surprising and far-fetched metaphors. In 1921, Borges joined up with his cousin Guillermo, his sister Norah, a few of the friends he had made in Spain and several would-be poets he had recruited back in Buenos Aires to launch the magazine *Prisma*, which appeared by being pasted up on walls around various locations in Buenos Aires overnight. Borges also entered Buenos Aires literary life more generally, joining the weekly *tertulia* of the famously unpublished writer and thinker Macedonio Fernández. Fernández, who is today enjoying something of a revival thanks to his connection with Borges, was a philosophical idealist and almost, we could say, a political nihilist. His fundamental belief in the unreality of the world and the non-existence of the self was to stay with Borges in one form or another for the rest of his life. During this period, Borges was also to publish his first volumes of poetry, *Fervor de Buenos Aires* (1923) and *Luna de enfrente* (1925), which were already beginning to show the effect of his move home in their evocation of the seldom-poeticized *arrabales* or poor inner districts of Buenos Aires. And a few years later, in a gesture that can only be read as a rejection of his previous avant-garde stance, Borges writes an eccentric biography of the little-known poet of the *barrios* Evaristo Carriego (1930), which is really a disguised love letter to the city of Buenos Aires.

As the 1920s turned into the 1930s, Borges slowly began establishing a small reputation. As he had earlier rejected his avant-gardism, so he now began to qualify the *criollo* nationalism that had marked his late twenties. He had begun to write for more mainstream newspapers and magazines, such as the daily *La prensa* and the weekly *El hogar*, working in a wide variety of styles and genres: book reviews, film reviews, gossip and what we would now call 'lifestyle items'. In fact, from his mid-twenties on, Borges had to make whatever meagre living he could from his journalism, and he wrote extraordinarily prolifically. It has been calculated, for example, that between 1936 and 1939 he reviewed some 208 books for *El hogar* alone. Altogether as a reviewer, he covered (and sometimes later translated) books by Woolf, Faulkner, Kafka, Poe and Chesterton, and was, as he once proudly wrote, the 'first traveller from the Hispanic world to set foot upon the shores of [James Joyce's] *Ulysses*' (*TL*, 12). (He was later to translate the last page of Molly Bloom's celebrated monologue for the magazine *Proa*.) He wrote on philosophy ('The Doctrine of Cycles'), religion ('A History of Angels'), linguistics and literature ('Narrative Art and Magic'), logic and mathematics ('The Perpetual Race of Achilles and the Tortoise') and the problem of a national literature ('The Language of the Argentines'). Borges was not only forming his own literary and philosophical system out of his engagement with all of this material, but also rethinking the notion of literature itself from the perspective of the review. Borges' essays and reviews were eventually collected in a series of books: *Inquisiciones* (1925), *Discusíon* (1932) and *Historia de la eternidad* (1936). Although considered failures at the time, they already show Borges taking liberties with the essay form: putting together widely disparate bodies of knowledge; including false or misleading references; and writing from an explicitly subjective point of view. Indeed, when Borges did finally turn to fiction in the book *Historia universal de la infamia* (1935) and the short story 'The Approach to Al-Mu-tasim' (1936), these took the form of fictitious life stories and a review of a book that did not exist, in a kind of revenge against the book reviews and capsule biographies of authors he was constantly having to write.

Undoubtedly, the most important literary connection Borges made during these years was with the magazine *Sur*, which was founded by the wealthy and cosmopolitan Victoria Ocampo in 1931. It was in this magazine (and later *Los anales de Buenos Aires*) that Borges began to publish his great fictions from the late 1930s on; and it was as a result of Ocampo's sponsorship that Borges was first translated into French, which was the beginning of his international fame. In May 1939, Borges published his first official story, 'Pierre Menard, Author of the *Quixote*', allegedly as an experiment to see whether he could still write after contracting an acute case of blood poisoning and hovering between life and death for several days in a hospital. As he was later famously – though falsely – to claim about the incident: 'I thought that if I tried to write a review and failed, I'd be through intellectually, but that if I tried something I had never done before and failed at that it wouldn't be so bad' (*A*, 154). From this point on, Borges continued to produce a stream of extraordinary stories for the magazine: 'Tlön, Uqbar, Orbis Tertius' in May 1940, 'The Circular Ruins' in December 1940, 'The Lottery in Babylon' in January 1941 and 'A Survey of the Works of Herbert Quain' in April 1941. These five stories,

'The Approach to Al-Mu'tasim', 'The Library of Babel' and the title story were published in a small volume entitled *El jardín de senderos que se bifurcan* [*The Garden of Forking Paths*], which came out on 30 December 1941. It is a volume that has been described by Borges biographer Emir Rodríguez Monegal as the 'single most important book of prose fiction written in Spanish in this century'.[1] The book, however, conspicuously failed to win a prize in the National Award for Literature, due at least in part to Borges' publicly stated political sympathies. From 1930 on, Argentina had been ruled by a succession of generals who assumed power after the economic downturn following the Wall Street Crash of 1929. The generals justified their rule, amidst a rising tide of fascism in Europe, through the appeal to 'Argentine' values. Borges, by this time, was thoroughly critical of his earlier aesthetics of *criollismo urbano* or urban realism. By 1931 he had already written the essay 'Our Inabilities', which was a sour look at the emerging nationalism in the arts. And, as the nationalist hysteria grew, he penned the powerful polemical text 'Yo, judío [I, A Jew]' (1934), in which he proudly claims a hypothetical Jewish heritage exactly against those nationalist anti-Semites who had accused him of hiding it.

The war years and those immediately following were difficult ones for Borges. On 4 June 1943, a group of right-wing and pro-Axis military officers masterminded the overthrow of the government of Ramón Castillo, on a platform of anti-British economic populism and the establishment of authentic *criollo* values. Under the generals, political parties were banned, trade unions were attacked and the press increasingly censored. Borges could only watch in horror as one of the young officers involved in the coup, the handsome and charismatic Juan Domingo Perón, proceeded to build himself a huge popular base among the workers and *descamidos* (the unemployed), undoubtedly in preparation for a future Hitler- or Mussolini-style Fascist Party. As well, Borges continued to grieve over the end of his relationship with the bohemian poet Norah Lange, which had finished as long ago as 1934, leaving him once again alone. Biographers even speak of two half-hearted suicide attempts in 1934 and 1940. It was a suffering accentuated by Borges witnessing the slow decline of his father, who had finally died blind and completely dependent on his wife in 1938. Borges himself was not yet blind, but his eyes had been getting steadily worse, and he knew very well the difficulties of life as a blind man without someone to help him. And yet it was also during these years that Borges would write some of the enduring masterpieces of his fiction: 'Death and the Compass' in May 1942, 'Funes, His Memory' in June 1942, 'The Theme of the Traitor and the Hero' in February 1944 and 'Three Versions of Judas' in August 1944. These stories and four others were gathered together under the title 'Artificios' and were then joined with the stories of *El jardín de senderos que se bifurcan* to become *Ficciones*, which was published on 4 December 1944. This time, both as a form of political protest against the government and as a way of making up for the embarrassment of snubbing *El jardín*, the members of the Argentine Society of Writers decided to give it a special award and to honour it with a celebratory dinner.

The European war ended in May 1945. Although Argentina was officially neutral, there was great sympathy for the Axis Powers within the government, and the country only belatedly came out for the Allies in March 1945, when victory was already assured. Borges, who followed developments overseas closely, wrote several fictions during the period dramatizing various aspects of the war. In 'The Secret Miracle' (1944), he takes up the story of a playwright who is arrested and sentenced to death, but is miraculously granted a year to complete his work. In 'Deutsches Requiem' (1946), he tells the story of a German camp commandant who seeks to drive mad a Jewish poet whose work he loves because it speaks to a part of himself he can no longer tolerate. In fact, immediately upon the conclusion of the War Borges was to write a defence of those British 'liberal' values to which he felt so close, applauding England for being the only country that was not 'fascinated with itself, that does not believe itself to be Paradise or Utopia' (*TL*, 213). It was a scepticism and self-questioning that always remained part of Borges' own personal ethos. In a much-quoted aphorism, he was once to declare of politics: 'Es una de las formas de tédio [It is one of the forms of tedium]'.[2] And later, when he briefly joined the Conservative Party in the early 1960s as a form of protest against Argentine politics at the time, he was to declare: 'If you are a conservative, you cannot be a fanatic, because one can't feel any enthusiasm about conservatism, any more than you can conceive of a fanatical conservative.'[3] It was an equanimity Borges was to need when Péron finally took power in a landslide victory in the elections held after the War in 1946 and just two months later Borges was sacked from his job as a shelver at the Miguel Cané Library, which had been the main source of income for him and his mother since the death of his father. Nevertheless, Borges continued to write his stories, according to many critics his greatest of all. Indeed, another important relationship, this time with the beautiful and communist-leaning writer Estela Canto, which had begun in late 1944, was now coming to an end, leaving Borges once again heart-broken; and two of his greatest stories of all – 'The Aleph' (1946) and 'The Zahir' (1947) – can be understood to be speaking of it in some way. The stories from this period – 'The Aleph', 'The Zahir', 'Emma Zunz' and 'The Immortal', amongst others – were collected in the volume *El Aleph*, which appeared on 26 June 1949. It was to be the last of Borges' undoubtedly major fictional texts.

It was during the 1950s that Borges' literary reputation really began to grow, both at home and abroad. Borges had first appeared in translation in 1939, thanks to his bilingual friend Néstor Ibarra, who published a translation of 'The Approach to Al-Mu'tasim' in the magazine *Mesures*. However, it was the French sociologist Roger Caillois, having heard of Borges through his lover Victoria Ocampo while stuck in Argentina during the War, whose recommendation got *Ficciones* accepted for the prestigious publishing house Gallimard in Paris in 1951. This and a selection from *El Aleph* entitled *Labyrinthes*, translated by Caillois himself in 1953, was soon to draw the attention of that generation of post-war French intellectuals who were to exert such an influence over not only the Francophone but also the English-speaking world just a few years later. As well, in Argentina itself the first book on Borges appeared in 1954, *Borges y la nueva generacíon* by Adolfo Prieto, and between 1957 and 1959 four more books on him were to appear. Ironically, though, it was around this time, when Borges began to receive his first serious critical attention in Argentina and his first recognition overseas, that his eyesight, which for a long time had not been good, suffered its final blow. By 1954 Borges had already undergone eight operations on his eyes; but during his annual holidays at Mar del Plata, where he was staying with his good friend and occasional literary collaborator Adolfo Bioy Casares and his wife Silvina Ocampo, he slipped on some rocks at the beach, and when he got up he realized that he could no longer see even through his remaining good eye. Thereafter, Borges' eyesight would be confined to only the roughest outlines of things, and he could no longer read or write in any sustained way. Those intricately composed stories for which he had become famous, in which he managed to conjure up an entire world in a few pages, would no longer be possible for him. Soon after *El Aleph*, Borges stopped writing fiction – he would not publish a new book of stories for some twenty-one years – and returned to writing poetry, which was easier to remember and could be dictated to a secretary. The last piece of writing by Borges that is truly essential to his reputation is his book of critical essays, *Otras inquisiciones*, which appeared in 1952 and is a collection of some 39 non-fiction pieces written over a period of 15 years, covering all manner of subjects, from small studies of favourite writers like Hawthorne, Wells, Whitman, Valéry, Chesterton and Shaw, to major pieces of literary criticism like 'Kafka and His Precursors' and innovative reworkings of the philosophical tradition like 'A New Refutation of Time'. The volume reveals not only the extraordinary range of Borges' reading, both literary and philosophical, but also the profound relationship between his fictional and non-fictional writings. In fact, reversing the usual priority between a great writer's fictions and his occasional essays, Borges biographer James Woodall argues that Borges' fictions must be understood as 'mirror images' of the essays.[4]

The 1960s and 1970s were decades of continued military intervention in the government in Argentina. After the eventual overthrow and exile of Péron in 1955, a series of army and army-backed governments was unable to restore order, and by the 1970s the country was effectively in a state of collapse. The ruling junta was continuously assailed by strikes and riots, and in 1970 the Péronist-inspired Montoneros guerillas kidnapped and executed the general who had orchestrated Péron's removal. At the same time, death squads, secretly authorized by the military, were conducting their own campaign of terror and torture. Altogether it is estimated that during the so-called Dirty War of the 1970s some 30,000 trade unionists and other left-wingers 'disappeared'. In 1973 Péron himself even returned from exile in Franco's Spain to attempt to restore stability, before the military in turn ousted his widow's government in 1976. During this time, Borges, although in principle supporting the same 'democratic regeneration' he had advocated when Péron was originally overthrown, gradually began to despair of the chances of democracy in Argentina. After all, it was democracy that had first elected and then re-elected Péron, his lifelong political enemy. In a subtle form of protest, Borges spent much of the two decades overseas, in a new career of picking up awards and honorary degrees and giving lectures to selected audiences. In 1961, he had shared the inaugural International Publishers' Prize with Samuel Beckett, as a result of which, as he said, 'my books mushroomed overnight throughout the western world' (*A*, 162). He travelled to and gave talks in Texas in 1961, London and Madrid in 1963, Berlin and Paris in 1964, Peru in 1965 and Italy and the east coast of America in 1967, just to mention the first few years of this incessant journeying. It was a period of truly world-wide celebrity for Borges, in which he cultivated his persona of a serene but slightly unworldly old man and offered elegant, slightly simplified versions of the themes of his stories in endless interviews. But it was also during this period that Borges could be said to have fallen out of favour with his original Latin American audience. He was never particularly encouraging towards that generation of writers from the region who came up after him, who saw their work as part of a wider Latin American social and political movement. He had always remained sceptical both of Castro's Cuba and of that great Argentine revolutionary icon Che Guevara. As well, in response to the ongoing Argentine political crisis, he made a series of ill-considered public statements to the effect that he would be prepared to countenance an 'enlightened dictatorship', if he could be sure that nothing like the Péron mistake would ever be repeated.[5] Most inexcusably, in 1976 he accepted a trumped-up award, the ludicrously named Grand Cross of the Order of Merit, from Chile, and even had lunch with its resident dictator Augusto Pinochet. It has been suggested that, because of this political error, the Nobel Prize was forever to be denied to Borges.

In 1975 Borges' mother, with whom he had lived virtually all of his seventy-six years, died. Borges was by now a frail blind man, who needed practical assistance in all aspects of his everyday life. During his many trips overseas, he had relied upon the assistance of a succession of young women, after his mother had become too old to accompany him. Borges had in fact had a brief and disastrous marriage with an old girlfriend in the 1960s; but a friendship gradually grew between him and a young woman who attended the informal classes he held in Anglo-Saxon at the National Library of Argentina, where as one of his honours he had been installed as Director after the original overthrow of Péron. In 1986, Borges and María Kodama married in Geneva, the place of his European schooling, and where Borges had gone to die, knowing that he had inoperable cancer of the liver. On 4 June 1986 Borges died. At the time he was widely regarded as one of the twentieth century's greatest writers, preceding and making possible a whole strain of post-war experimentation in the novel (Latin American Magic Realism, the French New Novel, American metafiction), and indeed one of the major predictors of and inspirations behind the whole cultural movement of post-modernism. He was also acknowledged as one of the principal influences on a whole generation of French structuralist and post-structuralist thinkers and on all the work in the humanities inspired in turn by them. Today, Borges is increasingly seen as a forerunner of post-colonial literature and as a prophet of the internet, cyberspace and computer games. Although Borges had been written about extensively while he was alive, his death brought about a comparative rush of publication, as the first academic specialization in his work became evident. Harvard University's library catalogue records some eleven new books on Borges in 1987 and the same number again in 1988. A number of memoirs and biographies had already been written about Borges during his lifetime, but several more appeared in the years following his death. Critics have continued to explore the literary allusions in and the literary influences upon Borges' writings. Books have appeared attempting to sketch the cultural and more specifically philosophical background to his work. As time goes on, intellectual fashions change, and there is an emphasis now not so much on the canonical short stories of the late 1930s and 1940s, but on the more realistic earlier and later poems and tales about the *compadres* or gangsters of the cities and the *gauchos* or cowboys of the countryside. There has been an emphasis too away from the fantastic and speculative in his work and towards its response to the social and political events that were occurring while he was writing. There has been a thinking as well of how the work understands itself in relation to the Western canon and how it might speak of its original Argentine situation. Borges lives on in the twenty-first century, no longer perhaps our contemporary; but his pastness, his strangeness, his foreignness, continue to strike us with renewed force.

\* \* \*

As we have seen, any number of critical approaches have been taken to the work of Borges: the tracing of his literary influences, the filling in of his philosophical background, even the psycho-analysis of his life in the search for clues to his literary impulses and motivations. It is the everyday business of scholarship, and contributes enormously to our understanding of his work. However, the only problem with this is that Borges' own work is a parody or travesty of such scholarly method; it mimics the form of the academic essay or report; it puts forward false facts and attributions; it seeks to undermine the assumptions of authorial intention and a stable meaning to the text. More precisely, Borges' work is *about* the methods used to interpret it; they find themselves the subject of the story they are trying to analyse. There is thus a subtle inadequacy about most critical methods in relation to Borges' stories, no matter how much the critic tries to take this into account or even make it the subject of their analysis. The critic applies a methodology the story already addresses, in a subtle begging of the question. Indeed, many of the traditional literary analyses of Borges can strike us as a kind of *avoidance* of his stories' most subversive aspects in their desire always to compare them to something else (a story, a writer, a philosophical system). For all of their interpreters' belief that they are revealing some hidden truth of Borges' stories in seeing them in relation to something else, this is largely what they fail to do. There is a kind of *limit*, we would argue, in applying the usual critical methods to Borges' stories, which is rarely acknowl-edged, but is as much as anything what the stories are about. There is something we miss in not being willing to read each story by itself, to see what it has to tell us in its own words, with-out resort to external reference. Borges' stories have their own internal resources that allow us to read them and that allow them to tell us how to read them.

Accordingly, then, we seek to do something here that has only rarely been attempted in all of the vast literature on Borges: simply to read a number of his stories with as much care and in as much detail as possible. Our readings here are not virtuosic, erudite or conceptually complex, but – qualities that Borges himself aimed at – sober, subtractive, exhibiting almost the absence of qualities. As early as 1926, Borges wrote in 'A Profession of Literary Faith': 'I have now conquered my poverty, recognizing among thousands the nine or ten words that get along with my soul' (*TL*, 27); and in perhaps the ultimate paradox of what we seek to do here what we discover, when we read each story singularly, is that each is saying the same thing. For what is finally at stake in Borges' stories is not a style or even a series of literary themes but a *logic* or *system*. What we see played out in the great Borges stories – in some more than others, but this is what makes some greater than others – is the coincidence of *the one and the many*. It is a logic that, according to Borges, is both literary and philosophical, or we could say that it represents the philosophical in literature and the literary in philosophy. Borges often speaks (or has often been understood to speak) of 'metaphysics as a branch of the literature of fantasy' (*CF*, 74), but what he properly means by this is the subjecting of philosophy to this 'literary' logic. It is a logic that we try to elaborate here in general terms, but it is also never to be seen outside of the stories. It is only to be played out 'fictionally', just as it is what takes Borges' stories beyond fiction towards something like philosophy. At once it is only to be found in the specific details of each story and it is a general template that allows us to read these details. In our emphasis on the great or canonical Borges stories here, and on the wider 'logic' or 'philosophical' basis of his text, there is undoubtedly something of a return to an 'original' Borges against all recent social-historical or post-colonial readings of him. It is possible, we claim, to read him again beyond all context, all biography, all literary and philosophical influence, just at that point when we might have thought this was a little passé, old-fashioned, even politically regressive or conservative. This, at least, is the hope of this *Reader's Guide*, which as much as possible simply wants to read ten of Borges' greatest stories, believing that they contain in themselves all of the astonishment, instruction and entertainment that we need.

## STUDY QUESTION 1

Critics have often argued that Borges' 'first' official story, 'The Approach to Al-Mu'tasim', creates the template for Borges' mature fiction. They particularly note that the equivalence spoken of at the end between 'the seeker and the sought' (*CF*, 87) is the key not only to the story but to Borges' work in general. We might note, however, that this equivalence, if implied at the beginning of the story, is deferred, never takes place by the end. In what ways is this impossible but necessary equivalence between the seeker and the sought – or, let us say, between the reader and what they read – the key to Borges' fiction? If the real subject to Borges' work is the *relationship between* the reader and the work, how does this relationship at once precede and come after any attempt to represent it?

## CHAPTER 2

# READING THE SHORT STORIES:
## THE LABYRINTHINE

Of the 'nine of ten words' that got along with Borges' soul, the word 'labyrinth' is undoubtedly the one with which he is most closely identified. It is an association that first begins, for English speakers at least, with the publication in 1964 of *Labyrinths*, which was a selection of stories and essays from *Ficciones*, *El Aleph* and *Otras Inquisiciones*. *Labyrinthe* was also the title chosen for the first German translation of Borges' writings, which appeared in 1959. In fact, as we know, *Labyrinthes* was the name originally given by Roger Caillois to his translation of Borges' writings into French in 1952. It was undoubtedly Caillois' decision that the English and German publishers of Borges followed, and that accounts for the emphasis on the notion of the labyrinth in at least the French- and English-language receptions of Borges' work. Interestingly enough, not only do none of the stories in the English-language edition of *Labyrinths* contain the word 'labyrinth' in its title, but the two stories from *El Aleph* that actually do were excluded. Indeed, 'labyrinth' does not enter Borges' lexicon in any serious way until the 1930s. The word is infrequently, if at all, used in the early poetry, and it is only by the time of the stories of *Historia universal de la infamia* and the critical essays of *Discusión* that 'labyrinth' is to be found consistently. By the end of Borges' career, however, the word is used almost continuously, no longer strictly necessary to the meaning of the text but more a verbal trademark or signature, as though to assure the reader that what they had before them was written by Borges. It is certainly possible to argue that the international reception of Borges in terms of the labyrinth retrospectively began to affect his work, and in his later years even Borges himself could declare that he was 'weary of labyrinths'.[1]

The word or concept 'labyrinth' is employed in a variety of ways throughout Borges' work. It is used to refer to a really existing object, as in the poem 'The Labyrinth' or the short story 'The House of Asterion'. It is used to describe objects that do actually appear to have labyrinth-like qualities, as in the poem 'Browning Resolves to Be a Poet', where Borges writes of 'red London labyrinths' (*SP*, 351), or the story 'The Other Death', where he writes of 'weaving labyrinths of marches' (*CF*, 224). Finally, it is used metaphorically to transfer labyrinthine qualities on to objects that are not usually thought of as labyrinth-like, as in the poem 'Alexandria, A.D. 641', where Borges writes of the 'solitary labyrinth of God' (*SP*, 393), or the story 'The End', where he writes of the strumming of a guitar as an 'inconsequential labyrinth, infinitely tangling and untangling' (*CF*, 168). And, of course, Borges' employment of the 'labyrinth', both as the subject of his poem and stories and as a narrative and stylistic device within them, has been much analysed. Critics have looked for the origins of Borges' fascination with the labyrinth, from his coming across an engraving of a labyrinth as a young boy to his later acquaintance with the artist Xul Solar, who painted de Chirico-like scenes of imaginary cities. They have searched for the cultural precedents Borges drew on when he took up the labyrinth in his own work, from the classical myth of Theseus and the Minotaur to Giovanni Battista Piranesi's famous *Carceri d'invenzione*, etchings of made-up gaols whose vistas appear to recede into infinity. Critics have even in a psychoanalytic vein interpreted Borges' obsession with the labyrinth in terms of an ongoing child-like fear of being separated from his mother.[2] Undoubtedly, the most sophisticated analysis of Borges' use of the labyrinth is Ana María Barrenechea's *Borges, the Labyrinth Maker* (1965), which compiles a list of the words with which labyrinth is most often associated in Borges (weave, intertwine, confuse), and thus the meanings the word accumulates throughout his work (drawing, representation, narratives with a key).[3] It is, of course, an approach carried on in more detail by the various dictionaries and concordances now devoted to Borges' work, which systematically list the various mentions of the word labyrinth in his writings and the range of purposes to which it is put.

But, before pursuing these researches, we must first ask another question. It is: what exactly *is* a labyrinth? In one sense, the question is easy to answer. When we speak of a labyrinth, we inevitably mean to refer either to the prison Daedalus built for King Minos on the island of Crete or to those topiaried hedges popular in European gardens throughout the eighteenth and nineteenth centuries. (In fact, scholars make a distinction between the maze, in which there are dead ends and misleading alternatives, as with hedges, and the labyrinth, in which we follow the twists and turns of a single path, as with the prison Daedalus built.[4]) But the question gets more difficult to answer when Borges can write of an 'infinite labyrinth' (*CF*, 124) or an 'inexhaustible labyrinth' (*CF*, 253), or can describe as 'labyrinthine' such things as time, space, human destiny and even the world itself. In the very ubiquity of the notion, it begins to lose its outlines, its ability to be defined. Perhaps, as Borges once suggested in an interview, in its omnipresence we are no longer able to say whether it exists or not. 'If we were positively sure that the universe is a labyrinth, we would feel secure. But it may not be a labyrinth.'[5] We would argue, however, that it is just this uncertainty as to whether it exists or not that *is* the labyrinth. At its deepest level, it is not simply that we are inside a labyrinth or that the labyrinth is equivalent to the world. It is rather that *we cannot know* whether we are inside a labyrinth, whether the labyrinth is the world. More than any physical object or qualifying characteristic, the labyrinth is a kind of *hypothesis* about the world. And the real split it introduces is not that between two paths within the labyrinth but that between the labyrinth and the world. It is this strange logic of the labyrinth that we take up here through a reading of two of Borges' stories: 'The Garden of Forking Paths' and 'The Immortal'.

## 'THE GARDEN OF FORKING PATHS'

'The Garden of Forking Paths', unlike many of Borges' stories, did not originally appear in a magazine, but was published for the first time in the collection of the same name in December 1941. It takes its place as the last story there, and we can say that Borges means to suggest by this not only that it was the last piece written for the volume, but that the idea of the end or finality is somehow at stake in it. More particularly, the story must be read as the continuation of another that appears before it in the collection, 'An Examination of the Works of Herbert Quain'. 'The Garden of Forking Paths' is undoubtedly one of Borges' most discussed and critically elaborated stories. Its central conceit of a literally 'labyrinthine' novel, in which, instead of choosing between various narrative alternatives, the author chooses all of them, has been tremendously influential, not only on the future development of the novel but also on cinema and philosophy. As early as the 1950s, such French New Novelists as Alain Robbe-Grillet were trying to realize Borges' ambition in a series of novels like *In the Labyrinth* (1959) and *The House of Assignation* (1965). Borges' suggestion was also taken up in such examples of American metafiction as Robert Coover's 'The Babysitter' (1969) and Richard Brautigan's *A Confederate General from Big Sur* (1969). The same idea of presenting all of the possible outcomes of an event without indicating which one is 'real' has also been explored in cinema, from Alan Resnais' *Last Year in Marienbad* (1961) to such recent Hollywood films as the Charlie Kaufman-scripted *The Eternal Sunshine of the Spotless Mind* (2004). The central notion of Borges' story has also been explored at the highest reaches of philosophy, with French philosopher Gilles Deleuze using the story to illustrate the concept of mutually inconsistent or non-compossible alternatives co-existing in his *The Fold: Leibniz and the Baroque* (1988). The story has also been investigated for its analogies to chaos theory and the many-worlds interpretation of quantum mechanics. Finally, its vision of endlessly branching links, each leading on to another, has been seen to predict such things as the internet and interactive computer games, in which the player can decide which narrative they want to follow.

The form 'The Garden of Forking Paths' takes is that of the spy or detective genre. The piece even won second prize in the annual *Ellery Queen's Mystery Magazine* contest in 1948. The story is said to be an excerpt from a confession by the Chinese agent Yu Tsun, who has been convicted of spying for the Germans during the First World War and awaits execution. The explanation of how Yu ended up in these circumstances begins with him ringing up his fellow conspirator Viktor Runeberg and realizing that the spy network for which he had been working has been penetrated, when an agent from the other side answers the phone. Yu must then figure out, in the time remaining before his capture, how to communicate the information he has obtained concerning the location of the new British artillery park on the Ancre River in France. Looking through the telephone book, he comes across someone bearing the same name as the town in which the artillery park is to be found. Barely eluding his pursuer, an Irishman named Richard Madden, Yu catches a train to the suburb where this person lives. Upon arriving at his stop, he is greeted by a group of youths, who seem to know without being told where he wants to go. 'Follow that road there to the left, and turn left at every crossing' (*CF*, 122), they advise him, which as Yu recalls is the preferred method for getting out of a labyrinth. Indeed, Yu, as he gets closer to his destination, enters into a series of reflections on his dead grandfather, Ts'ui Pen, a governor of the Yunan province back in China, who at a certain point withdrew from his career to write a novel and construct a labyrinth. Finally, Yu arrives at his destination, where he is greeted by the eminent sinologist Stephen Albert. Albert too seems to expect him, even if he mistakes him for Hsi P'eng, a Chinese diplomat with a name that sounds much like his grandfather's. 'You will no doubt want to see my garden?' (*CF*, 123) Albert asks Yu. Albert then explains that by this he means 'the garden of forking paths' (*CF*, 123), as he leads him along a meandering path around his house, in what we take to be the object to which the title of the story refers.

Once inside Albert's house, time appears to slow down. Yu decides that his 'irrevocable decision' (*CF*, 123) can wait. After taking a seat, Albert begins to explain to Yu the truth behind his grandfather's retirement, about which Yu had been meditating a moment before. Ts'ui said when he retired that he wanted to construct a book and a labyrinth, but all he left behind him after thirteen years of solitary labour was what seemed like the various drafts of a half-completed story, with all of its rethinkings and changes of mind left in. It appeared as though he had failed to complete both his book and his labyrinth. His family wanted the manuscript burnt, but a monk stepped in and had it published. The novel remained unread for many years, until one day Albert discovered the letter he now takes from his writing cabinet. It says simply: 'I leave to several futures (not to all) my garden of forking paths' (*CF*, 125). This was the clue Albert needed to reconstruct Ts'ui's ambition. What he suddenly realized was that Ts'ui's novel *was* the labyrinth he wanted to construct. The chaos and inconsistencies of the manuscript Ts'ui left behind were not the sign of any confusion or indecision, but intended by Ts'ui as the structure of his book. As Albert explains to Yu, in a famous passage:

> 'Almost instantly, I saw it – the garden of forking paths was the chaotic novel; the phrases "several futures (not all)" suggested to me the image of a forking in *time*, rather than in space. A full re-reading of the book confirmed my theory. In all fictions, each time a man meets diverse alternatives, he chooses one and eliminates the others; in the work of the virtually impossible-to-disentangle Ts'ui Pen, the character chooses – simultaneously – all of them. He *creates*, thereby, "several futures", several *times*, which themselves proliferate and fork. That is the explanation for the novel's contradictions. Fang, let us say, has a secret; a stranger knocks at his door; Fang decides to kill him. Naturally, there are various possible outcomes – Fang can kill the intruder, the intruder can kill Fang, they can both live, they can both be killed, and so on.' (*CF*, 125)

Albert goes on to say that what Yu's grandfather sought to construct was a labyrinth that was 'literally infinite', in which the choices between competing possibilities went on forever, and 'all the outcomes in fact occur' (*CF*, 125). And, as Albert explains all of this to Yu, Yu begins to feel within himself the 'pullulation' (*CF*, 126) of all these different times or possibilities of which Albert speaks. And yet, as Albert completes his explanation, this vision fades, and Yu sees coming down the path outside the house the relentless figure of Madden, who has finally caught up with him. For all of Albert's postulation of different times in which anything might happen, Yu resolves to complete the mission for which he had originally come. As Albert rises and turns, Yu shoots him in the back, killing him instantly. Madden bursts into the room, arresting Yu, but it is too late. Yu has calculated that news of the murder of the eminent sinologist will reach his chief back in Germany, and he will realize that the new British artillery park is in the town of Albert. Yu concludes his confession with the following satisfied thought:

> I have communicated to Berlin the secret name of the city to be attacked. Yesterday it was bombed – I read about it in the

same newspapers that posed to all of England the enigma of the murder of the eminent sinologist Stephen Albert. (*CF*, 127–128)

At the beginning of the story, the editor of what we read offers us a summary of what purports to be a passage from Liddell Hart's authoritative history of the First World War, in which Hart recounts the fact that an Allied offensive against the Serre-Montauban line, which had originally been planned for the 24 July, was postponed until the 29 July because of rain.

The suggestion for which 'The Garden of Forking Paths' is best known is that it is not only Ts'ui's book that can be seen to take the form of a labyrinth but also the wider world. At every moment of our lives we are moving through something like a labyrinth, in which we are confronted by a series of alternatives between which we have to choose, with each choice leading us further away from our starting point. What the story is said to remind us of is the way that a series of small decisions in the present, seemingly insignificant at the time, can produce wildly varying outcomes in the future. This is the brilliance of Borges employing the spy or detective genre for the outward form of his fiction. As opposed to the usual generic requirement that the spy or detective be an unthinking man of action, at several points in the narrative we become aware of the *lack* of necessity in the events we follow, the way they could easily have turned out otherwise. This can be seen, for example, in those moments in the text where the action slows down and Yu has the chance to observe things in their isolation and absence of meaning. We might think here of Yu's description of the 'usual rooftops' and of the fact that the day to come lacks 'all omens and premonitions' (*CF*, 120). Or we might think of his detailed enumeration of the contents of Albert's study, in which the narrative seems to come to a halt in an atmosphere of *symboliste* timelessness: 'The disk on the gramophone revolved near a bronze phoenix. I also recall a vase of *famille rose* and another, earlier by several hundred years, of that blue colour our artificers copied from the potters of ancient Persia' (*CF*, 123). There are also the different times of the memories or recollections that overtake Yu as he approaches Albert's house, and the distension or drawing out of time during his conversation with Albert. Finally, there are those several occasions of 'pullulation' (*CF*, 126, 127) that occur within Yu, in which he can literally feel those various possible futures competing within him.

But for all of the story's emphasis on the possibility that things might be otherwise, there is another equally strong thread that runs throughout it, which would have it that things were always destined to turn out the same. To begin with, Yu's confession is made under the shadow of a death sentence that has already been passed. And, from the outset, Yu is already thinking that this particular day will be the day of his 'implacable death' (*CF*, 120). Indeed, as he advises, when contemplating a difficult or unpleasant task like the one he proposes, it is best to imagine it as 'already done', to impose upon oneself 'a future as irrevocable as the past' (*CF*, 121). And the entire story is structured around a series of such repetitions between past and present: a foreigner kills Albert, as a foreigner killed Ts'ui; the British defeat the Germans, as one army defeated another in Ts'ui's novel . . . In fact, beyond even the series of conscious decisions that Yu makes in order to carry out his plan, there is a whole realm of unconscious motivations that also determines the action: Yu wants to prove to his German bosses the worthiness of someone of his race; Madden wishes to demonstrate to his English superiors the patriotism of the Irish. Finally, for all of Yu's efforts to change the course of the war by killing Albert, Hart tells us in the prologue to the story not only that the delay to the Allied offensive was caused by rain and not the bombing of the artillery park at Albert, but that this delay had no effect either on the specific battle or on the overall outcome of the War. Most ironically, in the last sentences of his confession Yu inadvertently reveals that his German bosses did not need Albert's death to know where the artillery park was: the news of the bombing was published in the *same issue* of the papers that reported Albert's death.

How, then, to reconcile these two seemingly opposed readings of the story? How to put together the idea that the story is about chance and contingency and the idea that it is about choice and predetermination? How is it possible that things might have turned out differently, while at the same time things had to turn out the same? In order to answer these questions, we might begin with the following consideration. When Ts'ui writes his letter announcing to the world his labyrinth, he does so in a way that leaves open the possibility that it might not be discovered: 'I leave to several futures (not to all) my garden of forking paths.' It is a caution that Albert repeats when he passes Ts'ui's labyrinth on to Yu. 'In all [times]', Yu says to Albert, 'I am grateful for, and I venerate, your recreation of the garden of Ts'ui Pen.' 'Not in all' (*CF*, 127), Albert corrects him, which is to say that not only is it not certain that in all futures will Yu be grateful to Albert, but that in some futures he will not even have a chance to be grateful because the labyrinth will not be discovered. But this is more complex than at first appears, for of course Albert would not even be able to express his doubts about the labyrinth existing unless the labyrinth *had actually been discovered*. And this necessity extends to Yu as well. With Albert dead, Yu now becomes the only one who knows the secret of his grandfather's labyrinth. Not only must Albert have discovered the principle behind this labyrinth, but he must have passed it on to Yu; and, with his own impending death, Yu must have passed it on to us. Again, for all of the multiple, infinitely branching alternatives the labyrinth is said to introduce into the world, they must all end in one point: the discovery and passing on of the labyrinth.

But this is not the end of the principle of the labyrinth. Although it does not change anything and all of its pathways end up at the same point, it *does* still introduce an alternative into the world. Although there is necessarily something outside of it, its eventual discovery that cannot be contingent, we can still speak of it as 'infinite'. In order to explain how this is so, we might turn to the story that precedes 'The Garden of Forking Paths' by two in Borges' original volume, 'A Survey of the Works of Herbert Quain'. In this story, Borges imagines a book by a fictitious author Herbert Quain entitled *April March*, in which a series of alternative scenarios all finish with the same conclusion. But *April March* must be understood as merely a literalization of the principle at stake in Quain's first book, *The God of the Labyrinth*, which is a detective novel. As the narrator explains, in this novel a first solution to a murder is given, but then just when we think everything is over a sentence is added at the end that forces us to re-read everything (*CF*, 108). All that we had thought had come about by accident we now see was a deliberate creation by the criminal in order to deceive us. It is not as though that first, incorrect solution can simply be done away with, for we would not have got to that second, correct solution without it. But this second solution explains not only the crime but also that first solution, showing how it is not outside of the events it seeks to explain but is part of them. And a number of Borges' own stories also have this structure, from 'Death and the Compass', in which the criminal deliberately entraps the detective by creating a series of false clues for him to follow (*CF*, 156), to 'The Theme of the Traitor and the Hero', in which enough evidence is left behind to reveal to a subsequent researcher the terrible truth behind an apparent act of heroism, but with the further calculation that the researcher will continue to propagate the official lie (*CF*, 146). In all of these cases, it is not so much the facts that are different with the addition of this second solution as the meaning behind these facts. The same set of facts is now read from a different point of view, as though behind the original narrative there was another that explains how it came about. It is as though that original set of events is doubled by another virtual possibility, so that at the same time as we move forward through the narrative another is opening up, revealing the truth behind how we got there. It is not some actual series of alternatives that confronts us at any moment, for the narrative can move forward only by making decisions and determining events in the only way it can. It is rather that every moment must be understood as standing in for another completely different explanation of events, which it precisely does *not* choose. And in truly spectacular detective stories, this process of finding a different explanation for the same material can be repeated almost endlessly. For any explanation of events there always seems to be opened up another, which takes into account not just these events but also how that first explanation forms part of them, needs itself to be explained for a reason entirely other than its own.[6] We might attempt to represent this diagrammatically:

$$\text{solution 2} \left\{ \begin{array}{c} \underbrace{\text{solution 1}} \\ \text{events} \end{array} \right.$$

It is this that we see in 'The Garden of Forking Paths'. Ts'ui's labyrinth is discovered, but this is to be understood not as a necessity without which we would not even know of the alternatives that the labyrinth introduces, but as itself one of the labyrinth's alternatives. That 'end' that seems to be outside of the labyrinth is now seen to be inside of it, only one of the many different 'ends' made possible by the labyrinth. And we see this detective-like effect of proposing different possible solutions to the same series of facts throughout 'The Garden of Forking Paths'. To take the most obvious example, just as with that added paragraph in *April March*, Albert goes back to Ts'ui's labyrinth armed with his letter to 're-read' its apparent chaos and finds that it was not accidental. Or the editor of the story in a footnote inserted towards the beginning seeks to refute the allegation that Madden simply murdered Runeberg, arguing that he shot him only in self-defence. Even, we might argue, this whole obscure episode involving Ts'ui's labyrinth is the secret explanation of the War, that it is not Hart's account that frames Yu's actions but Yu's actions that frame Hart's account. And yet each time the previous solution is shown to be amongst the events to be explained, this would be only from the point of view of another such 'solution'. If everything is subject to the labyrinthine logic of being only one of several possibilities, this is only to say that the labyrinth itself is necessary. And it is for this reason that the labyrinth is truly 'infinite'. Just like Scheherazade in *1001 Nights*, who endlessly defers her death by telling the story of how she ended up in front of the King telling her story, so each new engagement with the labyrinth is a retelling of the engagement before. It takes the previous explanation of events and shows that it was only ever one of two alternatives, that the path it chose was precisely not to choose another. The infinity of the labyrinth is not that of infinitely many alternatives confronting us at once between which we cannot choose, but that of one alternative after another so that we never finish choosing. It is the infinity of what we might call *always one more*.

### 'THE IMMORTAL'

Borges writes another story that involves the notion of the labyrinth not only in the literal sense but in the more complex sense we are trying to bring out here. It is 'The Immortal', which was originally published in *Los anales de Buenos Aires* in February 1947 and then included in *El Aleph*. It is a long story for Borges, coming in at some 6,500 words and made up of four different sections, along with a framing prologue, a retrospective reflection by the narrator and a (post-dated) postscript. It is also an extremely ambitious story, featuring a number of complex and easily misunderstood literary effects. First of all, although it is amongst those Borges stories in which the fate of the protagonist is meant to affect us, the central character here is vague and featureless, and the narrative style deliberately flat and low-key. Second, there are an enormous number of literary quotations and allusions scattered throughout the text. Although they can be justified – the critic Ronald Christ in his study *The Narrow Act: Borges' Art of Allusion* spends some thirty pages discussing them – they nevertheless run the risk of unnecessarily slowing down the narrative.[7] Last, Borges seeks to bring about a deliberate confusion of narrative voice in his text, with the result that we can never be entirely sure who is speaking. Not only are a number of Greek expressions used by a speaker who is meant to be Roman, but in a final narrative revelation we learn that the person we thought was narrating the story was not the narrator at all. Nevertheless, for all of the critics' reservations as to the final success of the story, 'The Immortal' is almost universally acknowledged as one of Borges' major works and an essential addition to the canon. If, as we will see, one of the aims of the story is to make clear the long tradition of depicting immortality that has existed throughout the West, it is also true to say that Borges' own version is one of the twentieth century's definitive interpretations, and has inspired, in turn, others to take up its themes. Alain Robbe-Grillet wrote and directed a film, *L'immortelle* (1963), which plays on many of the same narrative ambiguities as Borges' text. The character Melquíades, who keeps on coming back to life in Gabriel García' Marquez's *One Hundred Years of Solitude* (1967), is clearly a reference to Borges' central character. Finally, in 2007 as part of the United Kingdom's Architecture Week, artist Michelle Lord built her interpretation of the 'City of Immortals' described in Borges' story, as an example of what she called 'dream architecture'.

'The Immortal' begins in 1929 with the rare book dealer Joseph Cartaphilus selling to the Princess de Lucinge a copy of Alexander Pope's six-volume translation of Homer's *Iliad*. Cartaphilus is described as an emaciated and grimy-looking man, with grey eyes, grey beard and 'singularly vague' (*CF*, 183) features, and speaking several languages fluently but poorly. Inside the last volume of the Princess' copy of the *Iliad*, she finds a manuscript, which purports to tell the adventures of a Roman centurion, Marcus Flaminius Rufus, who lived during the reign of the Emperor Diocletian in the third century. Rufus is a tribune in one of the Emperor's armies, and early one morning while his forces are stationed in Egypt, a bloodied man rides towards him from out of the distance and speaks just before dying of a river that 'purifies men of death' (*CF*, 184). Rufus resolves then to go in search of this legendary river, which is said to lie 'at the ends of the earth' (*CF*, 184). His commanding officer grants him some 200 soldiers to begin his expedition; but, made feverish by the desert moon and driven mad by drinking poisoned water, they soon start to desert him. Eventually, Rufus leaves his camp with only a few of his most trusted men, but in time he becomes separated even from them. Wandering though the desert alone, and in sight finally of the fabled City of the Immortals, he collapses. When he awakes, he finds himself lying in a makeshift grave with his arms tied behind his back. Burning with thirst, he drags himself with enormous effort down a slope towards a small, dirty stream he notices trickling though the mud and plunges his head down to drink. Just before passing out, he notices himself inexplicably reciting a few words of Greek: 'Those from Zeleia, wealthy Trojans, who drink the water of dark Aisepos.' (*CF*, 186).

Coming to again, with his hands still tied behind his back, Rufus spends days and nights on the blazing sands unable to move. The strange dog-like creatures, who live in the surrounding caves and whom he had seen earlier on his journey, neither attack him nor come to his aid, despite his pleas for help. Eventually, Rufus frees himself and crosses the stream to enter the City of the Immortals, accompanied by two or three of these Troglodytes. When he crosses the City walls, he has then to negotiate an almost endless series of underground rooms, in which all but one of nine doors leads back to the same room. After a journey that seems to him interminable, Rufus reaches a final room, where a ladder takes him up to the City itself. The City in turn reveals itself to be another labyrinth, laid out seemingly randomly, with corridors that lead nowhere and staircases that peter out after two or three levels. There appears to be no consistent plan or design, with the most heterogeneous styles and functions yoked together without any thought. Almost in horror, Rufus flees the City, once again having to negotiate the series of underground chambers. There to greet him when he finally emerges is one of the Troglodytes who had earlier followed him. This particular Troglodyte accompanies Rufus on his subsequent journeys; and Rufus calls him Argus, after the dog in Homer's *Odyssey*. Rufus, as he gets to know him, is led to remark on how different their respective experiences must be. But one day, as a heavy rain falls on both of them, Rufus is astonished to see Argos lift his face to the sky and utter the words: 'Argos, Ulysses' dog' (*CF*, 190). When Rufus then asks him how much of the *Odyssey* he knows, Argos replies to Rufus' further amazement: 'Very little. Less than the meagerest rhapsode. It has been eleven hundred years since last I wrote it' (*CF*, 190).

At this point, Rufus not only realizes that the lowly Troglodytes are in fact the legendary Immortals, but begins to think through, aided by Argos, the logical consequences of immortality. He understands now why the Troglodytes were so indifferent to his suffering when they saw him lying for days in the sun with his arms behind his back after he had drunk from the stream that conferred eternal life upon him. It was not merely because they knew he would not be hurt, but also because of a kind of moral indifference in which all acts become equivalent to each other. As Rufus explains:

> Taught by centuries of living, the republic of immortal men had achieved a perfection of tolerance, almost of disdain. They knew that over an infinitely long span of time, all things happen to all men. As a reward for his past and future virtues, every man merited every kindness – yet also every betrayal, as reward for his past and future iniquities. Much as the way in games of chance, heads and tails tend to even out, so cleverness and dullness cancel and correct each other. Perhaps the rude poem of *El Cid* is the counterweight demanded by a single epithet of the *Eclogues* or a maxim from Heraclitus. The most fleeting thought obeys an invisible plan, and may crown, or inaugurate, a secret design. I know of men who have done

evil in order that good may come of it in future centuries, or may already have come of it in centuries past. (*CF*, 191)

Indeed, drawing the final consequence of this balancing out of opposites, some time in the tenth century the Immortals realize that, if there is a river whose waters confer immortality, there must also be a river whose waters restore *mortality*. Given that the number of rivers in the world is not infinite, it is certain that in the infinite amount of time available to them an Immortal will find that river. The Immortals then set out across the world in order to find the water that will bring an end to them.

The rest of the story details the wandering of Rufus, who like those other Immortals constantly searches for this second river. In 1066, he fights at the Battle of Hastings. In the thirteenth century, he translates the story of Sinbad in Egypt. In 1638, he is in Rumania and later in Germany. In 1714 in Aberdeen, he subscribes to the six-volume set of Pope's translation of the *Iliad*. In 1921, finally, a boat taking him to Bombay runs aground on the Eritrean coast. While ashore, he drinks water from an unidentified stream; and, upon pricking himself with a thorn, notices himself bleed and feel pain. He realizes with a sense of relief that he is once again mortal. Rufus' narrative then comes to a halt; and when he resumes a year later, he realizes, upon re-reading his manuscript, that what he has written seems unreal to him because 'the experiences of two different men are intermingled in it' (*CF*, 193). He notes that, while some of his statements would accord with a soldier like Rufus, much of what he has written seems as though written by a poet. In particular, he observes that sprinkled throughout the text are phrases and expressions taken from Homer. Not only do we as readers already suspect that the real author of the pages we have just read is Cartaphilus, but Rufus/Cartaphilus begin to suspect – although this is never explicitly spelled out – that not only have they once met Homer but that they actually *are* Homer. This accounts for the fact that the narrator expressly mentions that they once subscribed to Pope's *Iliad*. It would indeed be 'pathetic' (*CF*, 194), in the sense of moving, that Homer would find a version of his own tale in such a foreign place and in such a different tongue. It would also be appropriate that, insofar as he was Homer, Cartaphilus the bookseller ensured the perpetuation of Homer's *Iliad* by passing

on Pope's translation of it to another. It is perhaps no coincidence
that Cartaphilus dies at sea while returning to his homeland of
Smyrna and is buried on the island of Ios in the Aegean, because
these places are said to be where Homer was born and where he
was buried.

Critics have predominantly interpreted 'The Immortal' in
terms of Borges' long-held fascination with the 'nothingness of
personality'. It is the idea that, at certain moments in our lives,
we are able to go beyond our own individuality and enter into a
realm that is common to all.[8] We see this in Borges' argument
that in the act of copulation we are all the same person, or that
when we read Shakespeare we actually become Shakespeare
(*TL*, 323). It is not unrelated to the notion, also discussed by
Borges, that if we could but properly understand just one flower –
but any object would do – we would understand everything,
insofar as the flower contains or reflects like a mirror the entire
universe (*TL*, 240). It is an impersonality or universality of experience that is understood to come variously from the doctrines
of pantheism, Buddhism or even Spinoza, and has even been
explained autobiographically in terms of a revelation Borges
once had that he did not exist. And it is an impersonality that
absolutely guides Borges' literary practice. As opposed to seeing
literature as the expression of a singular individual, Borges
understands it as an anonymous, corporate exercise, unimaginable without the collaboration of everyone who reads and writes.
This is the point behind the series of literary quotations and
allusions Borges weaves throughout 'The Immortal'. Beyond
any particular meaning or source he wants to draw our attention
to, he is also making the point that the story of immortality *is*
immortal: that it originates with no one and lives on in being
transmitted from one storyteller to the next. (If Homer's Ulysses
is the original immortal, it must be remembered Homer himself
was merely formalizing a literary tradition that had existed a
long time before him.)

And yet for all of the compelling nature of this reading of
'The Immortal' as the expression of a philosophical doctrine or
as the outcome of some autobiographical experience, it still does
not go far enough in penetrating the inner logic of the story
itself. In order to do so ourselves, let us begin with that passage
in the text in which the narrator elaborates the consequences

of immortality. As opposed to the acts of a mortal, which are 'precious' and 'pathetic' insofar as they are selective, for an Immortal 'all things happen to all men'. It is a matter not of choosing to bring about any desired outcome, but of simply relying on the workings of chance. Over the infinite period of immortality, events 'cancel and correct' each other. For any particular thing that takes place, so too does its opposite. Thus an immortal might do evil so that 'good may come of it in future centuries, or may already have come of it in centuries past'. And, as the Immortals soon conclude, this also implies that, insofar as there is a stream in the world that confers immortality, there must be another that restores mortality. And, given that the number of streams in the world is not infinite and that immortals have an infinite amount of time to look, the Immortals are certain eventually to find this stream. Now, this might appear as though the immortal must do an infinite number of things, that everything must find its opposite, *before* the second stream can be found. It would be as though the search for this stream involves a literally endless journey, crossing all the countries in the known world, as it is depicted in the story. But, if we think about it, for an Immortal, who has an infinite amount of time on their hands, any *finite* period of time, no matter how long, would seem like only a brief moment. From an immortal perspective, at least, the finding of that second stream is almost instantaneous. It can occur at any time, whether 'all things' have already been done or not.

Indeed, we might even say not that there is an infinity of things that have to be done before that second stream is discovered, but that this infinity comes about only *after* that second stream is discovered. For, if we read the story closely, we notice that immortality exists only as a retrospective effect of being mortal, can be spoken of only *after* one has become mortal. This is what the narrator means when he says: 'There is nothing very remarkable about being immortal . . . What is divine, terrible and incomprehensible is *to know* oneself immortal' (*CF*, 191). It is to say that more than simply being known or not, immortality exists only *insofar as* it is known, and that this can be done only from the point of view of a mortal. We see this with the episode with Argo, where he realizes he is Homer only after the rain (his second stream) falls on his face. It also appears that Rufus' account was written only retrospectively after he too became mortal: it is notable that nowhere while he describes himself living among the Immortals does he admit to being immortal himself; that 'pathetic' quality he says characterizes aspects of his account is not merely the pathos of the poet but also that of mortality as such. It is possible as well that the manuscript hidden inside the Princess' copy of Pope was written by Cartaphilus only after he became mortal . . . For all of the infinite number of things that an Immortal is said to do in their life, drinking water from that second stream must be one of them. If in one way they discover this second steam only after doing an infinite number of things, in another this infinity exists only because it comes to an end thanks to this second stream. Indeed, it might be suggested that the Immortal does not even do an infinite number of things before drinking from that second stream, because he would not then get around to doing so, and he could not therefore become immortal. We have here the same situation as in 'The Garden of Forking Paths', in which for all of the alternative possibilities thrown up by the labyrinth one of them must include the discovery of the labyrinth itself. As there, the condition of immortality in 'The Immortal' changes nothing. Immortals do not even necessarily live longer than mortals, because they can come across that second stream any time. Indeed, pushing this logic of immortality a little further, we might even propose that we die only because we *are* immortal, that it is only because of the infinite amount of time that immortality grants us that we are certain to find that second stream.

It is at this point, finally, that we grasp the true logic of immortality and how it reproduces that of the labyrinth. The immortal discovers the second stream, it is said, because all things 'cancel and correct' each other in the state of immortality. But, as we have seen, if this second, mortalizing stream is found as a consequence of immortality, it also brings about immortality. Immortality does not exist until *after* that second stream has been found. In this sense, drinking from that second stream is the only act *not* covered by immortality, that is not sure to happen, insofar as immortality arises as a result of it. And perhaps by this drinking of water from the second stream we mean the *narration* of immortality, for again without this narration immortality would not exist. That is, at the same time as this drinking from the second stream represents a certain 'cancelling and correction', comes about as the opposite of what has occurred before, it must also be itself 'cancelled and corrected' by an opposite that has not yet occurred. This is the complicated logic behind the narrator's claim that the Immortals do evil so that good either will occur in the future or can be seen to have happened in the past. It is to suggest that every act is *both* good and bad, at once a repetition of what comes before and different from it. And this is also what is at stake in the narrator saying that every act is an 'echo of others that preceded it in the past . . . and that will repeat it in the future' (*CF*, 192) and that 'all things happen to all men'. It is again to suggest that each act is *both* the same *and* different, at once the cancelling and correction of another and having itself to be cancelled and corrected by another. And the final point here is that every moment is both mortal and immortal. For we could no sooner propose immortality as the end in its cancelling and correction of opposites than we would need another to cancel and correct *this* end, insofar as it is only from another, later point in time that this cancelling and correction could be seen. Each moment is at once the moment of our death – the attempt to take the place of that moment at the end of time in which opposites cancel and correct each other – and the deferral of this end – the cancelling and correction of a previous cancelling and correction. We might attempt to represent this diagrammatically:

$$\text{mortality} \left\{ \begin{array}{c} \text{mortality} \\ \overbrace{\qquad\qquad} \\ \text{immortality} \end{array} \right.$$

It is for this reason that 'The Immortal', like 'The Garden of Forking Paths', is about *time*. In 'The Garden of Forking Paths', Albert in deciphering Yu's labyrinth speaks of time as being its real subject. Everything stands in for time, is not to choose time, despite it never being mentioned there. As Albert says:

To *always* omit one word, to employ awkward metaphors and obvious circumlocutions, is perhaps the most emphatic way of calling attention to that word. It is, at any rate, the tortuous path chosen by the devious Ts'ui Pen at each and every one of the turnings of his inexhaustible novel. (*CF*, 127)

And, in a sense, time *is* this virtuality, that which cannot be grasped as such, although everything stands in for it. Time is labyrinthine, in exactly that sense we have tried to make clear. For let us think about time and how Ts'ui's novel resembles it. Our usual conception of time is that it is something like a series of points strung along a line, with one 'now' or moment succeeding another in unbroken succession. It is this succession that is or gives time. But we might ask: in what *time* does this succession take place? When does this substitution of one moment for another actually occur? If the second moment has to appear to allow the first to disappear, then we would end up having all moments at once, and time would come to a standstill. If the first has to disappear to allow the second to appear, then we would end up having a gap or hole in time, and we could never get from one moment to the next. In fact, for the linear unwinding of time to be possible, that first moment must disappear *as* the second moment appears. Running alongside actual time, in which one moment *succeeds* another, there must be another virtual time, in which two moments exist *at the same time*. Each moment takes the place of this virtual time, allowing it to become the second; but, in doing so, there is opened up another virtual time, which allows that second to appear. In this sense, we might say that the successive unwinding of time is just the perpetual falling short of an end that has already arrived. And we see the same thing in 'The Immortal', where we cannot get to the end, that is, drink from that second stream, because an infinity of actions must be completed before we get there. However, if in one way we cannot get to the end because an infinity of actions must first be completed, in another way this infinity arises only after we have already got to the end. As we saw with the idea of the same action being both good and evil, a repetition of what comes before and different from it, it is only because we are already at the end that we cannot get there; it is only within the same moment there is implied an infinite distance.[9]

This, to conclude, is how the question of narrative in 'The Immortal' must be understood. The logic of immortality is that we cannot die until everything has been 'cancelled and corrected', matched up with its opposite and equal. It entails the finding of that second stream, which at once mortalizes and allows immortality to be realized. And it is precisely of this discovery that we read in 'The Immortal', which in each of its parts is the story of how its various characters finds that second stream: Homer in the rain, as told by Rufus; Rufus with a stream near the coast of Eritrea, as told by Cartaphilus; and Cartaphilus at sea on the way home to Smyrna, as told by the narrator . . . And yet each of the narratives that tells of the death of an Immortal lives on after it as a kind of excess or remainder. In other words, this narrative that cancels and corrects must itself be cancelled and corrected before its narrator can die. The logic here is exactly like the one we saw in 'The Garden of Forking Paths', in which the solution that reveals the labyrinth necessarily opens up the possibility of another coming along after it and showing how it is *part of* the labyrinth. Each successive narrator here in 'The Immortal' – Homer, Rufus, Cartaphilus, Borges – in a sense narrates the death of the narrator before, who in turn has narrated the death of the narrator before him. What we have in the various sections that make up the narrative is not merely a series of successive episodes in the same story, but a series of stories within stories. Each story tells the story of the Immortal before, showing how their narrative produces an excess that has to find its opposite before its narrator can die. Like the 'infinite labyrinth' of Scheherazade, in 'The Garden of Forking Paths' (*CF*, 126) immortality is always a certain narration of narration. There is no original immortality – not even Homer's – because immortality always begins with the narration of the death of a previous Immortal. Immortality, in other words, is not an infinity without end, but rather an endless series of mortalities, each of which proposes another end. It is not a set of narratives one after the other, but rather what we might call an endless series of post-scripts, each of which is *about* the other. Immortality is the very passing on of the story of immortality. It exists only in the very passage from one to another. This is why we might say, despite the title of Borges' story, there is never only one immortal, but always at least two. The 'experiences of two different men are intermingled in it', if we mean by that the experiences of both mortality and immortality.

## STUDY QUESTION 1

As Barbara Alfano ('Fugitive Diegesis of the First Person Singular in Borges and Calvino', *Variaciones Borges* 11 (2001), pp. 103–119) and other critics have made clear, part of Borges' narrative strategy in 'The Immortal' is to render unclear who is speaking by shifting between the first person ('Que yo recuerde', *OC* I, 533; 'divisé', *OC* I, 534) and the third person ('ofremos', *OC* I, 533; 'Partimos', *OC* I, 534) in its mode of address. For Spanish-speaking students, identify other places in the original text where Borges does this. Then compare the relative success of Andrew Hurley in *Collected Fictions* and James Irby in *Labyrinths* in conveying this strategy in the English.

## STUDY QUESTION 2

The critic Jaime Alazraki speaks of a certain 'oxymoronic structure' to Borges' essays (in Dunham and Ivask, *The Cardinal Points of Borges*). What are some of the examples of this 'oxymoronic structure' in the Borges stories we have looked at here? Why does Borges employ this oxymoronic structure? Does it lead to a general form of scepticism, a 'cancelling and correction' of opposites, or can it be read another way?

## CHAPTER 3

# READING THE SHORT STORIES: THE BORGESIAN

As with any great writer, it is tempting to try to say what makes Borges who he is. Why is he worth reading? What particular set of qualities does he bring to literature? How does he relate to other authors? Accordingly, in the vast literature on Borges, there have been many attempts to identify the distinguishing characteristics of Borges. Critics have sought, on the stylistic level, to analyse his peculiar vocabulary and mode of expression. They have complied lists of those 'nine or ten' words that accord with his soul: infinite, circular, universe, the colour red. They have spoken of his habit of choosing unexpected and etymologically precise adjectives: 'unanimous' to qualify 'night' (*CF*, 96); 'interminable' to qualify a 'brick wall' (*CF*, 256). Critics have sought to speak more generally of Borges' style, which is notable for bringing an English concision to the grandiosity of literary Spanish. Borges' most recent translator notes Borges' frequent use of the semi-colon to replace the 'ands', 'buts' and 'thens' that usually link sentences.[1] The Mexican writer Carlos Fuentes speaks of Borges' 'dazzling prose, so cold it burns one's lips'.[2] On a still more general level, critics have sought to elaborate Borges' particular narrative strategies and preferences. These range from Borges beginning a story as though it were a review of a book to treating his own text as though it were an entry in an encyclopaedia. Critics speak as well of a certain 'thinness' to Borges' style, in which only selected moments from the events in question are given and everything is directed towards the final narrative revelation, with none of that excess of detail that produces the effect of the 'real' in fiction.[3]

On a still larger scale, critics have attempted to identify the broader ideas that animate Borges' fiction. These are, in part, that series of words we find throughout Borges' texts; but they are also the more abstract, amorphous concepts that do not always directly feature there: time, heroism, the reversal of fate, the unreality of the world. It is the interplay of these concepts that can be understood to form the 'cardinal points' of Borges' universe and to give his work its underlying force. There is then the wider culture that Borges' work both comes out of and is a response to. This is that staggeringly diverse group of writers and thinkers whose work Borges is said to have been influenced by or to have otherwise encountered at some point in his career. This would include not only those writers with whom Borges bears some affinity (Chesterton, Shaw, Wells, Stevenson), but also those who exert a pressure on his work in their difference from it (Joyce, Woolf, Faulkner, James). This series would also include particular philosophers, scientists and mathematicians whose works Borges read, or at least read about, and frequently made the basis for his stories: Zeno, Berkeley, Hume, Cantor. And, alongside all of this, the focus of much of the last twenty or thirty years of Borges scholarship is the question of Borges' general cultural situation. This is before all else to ask how everything spoken of above is mediated through Borges being Argentine. How did the fact that Borges comes from a faraway, provincial culture affect how he responded to the various cultural influences he came into contact with? How is his work to be seen not as an imitation of the European canon, but as an active response to it? In what ways does Borges speak of location in his work, beyond any obvious geographical reference?

All of these efforts to analyse Borges stylistically and thematically, to identify his literary and philosophical sources, to situate him and his work within wider social and historical forces, are absolutely essential to any consideration of him. We could not imagine a proper response to Borges that did not attempt to say what his particular contribution to literature was, what he managed to achieve that no one else had previously. To look at the various attempts by critics to undertake this is important at least in understanding the history of the reception of Borges, the way he has successively been taken up over time. And yet, as we outline in Chapter 1, there is a *limit* to these approaches, insofar as Borges' work constitutes a questioning of the assumptions behind them. Not only Borges' literary criticism, but also his stories ask how we can speak of what is unique or distinctive about a particular author. What is the connection between an author and what they write? What is the relationship between an author and the cultural and geographical context in which they work? In other words, Borges is not only *subject to* the methods of literary criticism, but also *subjects* these methods to critical interrogation. He blurs the boundaries between fiction and criticism not only in introducing the methods of criticism into fiction but also in 'fictionalizing' criticism. And this is to say that he does not so much parody or satirize it as show that the logical assumptions underlying it are 'fictional', cannot entirely be demonstrated. However, if Borges makes it difficult to speak about him in challenging most of the usual ways of speaking about an author, it is *Borges* himself who does this. It is this challenge to or inversion of the conventional categories of criticism that *is* perhaps the 'Borgesian' in literature. It is this category of the Borgesian that we seek to take up here through a reading of three of Borges' texts: 'Kafka and His Precursors', 'Pierre Menard, Author of the *Quixote*' and 'The Library of Babel'.

## 'KAFKA AND HIS PRECURSORS'

The essay 'Kafka and His Precursors' first appeared in the newspaper *La Nación* on 19 August 1951, and was subsequently published in *Otras inquisiciones* [*Other Inquisitions*]. *Other Inquisitions* is a collection of essays notable for the extremely wide variety of topics addressed, which points either to the wide-ranging nature of Borges' interests or to the contingencies of book reviewing. Certainly, reading the pieces in the order in which they appear in the book, we are forced to ask whether there is any one reader for whom all of these subjects could be meaningful. But 'Kafka and His Precursors' is already *about* such questions, the varied assortment in which it finds itself. The essay takes the form of that classic academic practice of listing an author's influences as some way of explaining what makes them who they are. As with so many of Borges' exercises in this form, the essay can be understood as a parody or satire. However, the humour masks a serious point. The subject of the essay is the great Czech writer Franz Kafka, the author of such acclaimed masterpieces as *The Castle*, *The Trial* and 'Metamorphosis'. Kafka was certainly a writer who meant a great deal to Borges. Borges applied the adjective 'Kafkaesque' to several of his stories, and invented the phonetically similar word 'Qaphqa'

(*CF*, 104) in the story 'The Lottery of Babylon' to refer to a sacred latrine. Indeed, Borges even translated Kafka's famous parable 'Before the Law' immediately before his own period of major fiction-making. In the end, 'Kafka and His Precursors' is not so much a parody or satire as a literary manifesto or even an act of autobiography. Appearing in the guise of literary criticism, the essay is perhaps as close as Borges ever got to declaring his own literary methods and inspirations. The essay is certainly an almost perfect demonstration of the particular form of logic that runs throughout Borges' work, of that which makes it 'Borgesian'.

'Kafka and His Precursors' does indeed begin with all the outward appearances of a conventional academic essay. Borges writes:

> At one time I considered a study of Kafka's precursors. I had thought, at first, that he was as unique as the phoenix of rhetorical praise; after spending a little time with him, I felt I could recognize his voice, or his habits, in the texts of various literatures and various ages. (*TL*, 363)

Borges then proceeds to list the six precursors he has so far identified. The first is the pre-Socratic philosopher Zeno, who put forward a series of arguments supposedly refuting motion. Zeno argued that for an object to get from A to B, it must first cross a point C, half-way between them; and to get to from A to C, it must first cross a point D, half-way between them; and so on. The logical consequence is that motion is impossible because there would always be another point half-way between where we were and where we wanted to get to. The second is the ninth-century Chinese author Han Yu, who argued that the unicorn is hard to classify because, although it is like a horse, insofar as it has a mane, and like a bull, insofar as it has a horn (and even like the wolf and deer), it is not exactly like any of them. The third is the theologian Søren Kierkegaard and the parable he tells about Danish clergymen telling their parishioners that a trip to the North Pole is good for their souls. Actual trips to the North Pole being difficult to undertake, however, these clergymen end up declaring that 'any journey – from Denmark to London, say, in a steamship, or a Sunday outing in a hackney coach – could be seen as a veritable expedition to the North Pole' (*TL*, 364). The fourth is the poet Robert Browning and his poem 'Fears and Scruples', which tells the story of a man who believes he has a famous and noble friend and shows this friend's letters to others. When these others cast doubt on this friend's nobility and even on the genuineness of the letters, the man replies: 'What if this friend happened to be God?' (*TL*, 364). The fifth precursor is the late-nineteenth-century French novelist Léon Bloy and one of the stories from his *Histoires désobligeantes*, which concerns a group of would-be travellers, who accumulate atlases, train schedules and suitcases, but who die without ever leaving the town in which they were born. And the sixth precursor Borges adduces is the opposite of this. It is the twentieth-century English writer Lord Dunsany and his poem 'Carcassone', in which an army of warriors sets out from an enormous castle for Carcassone; but, despite crossing mountains and encountering monsters, they never reach their destination, although they do once glimpse it from afar.

In each case here, Borges selects an author who reveals to us something of Kafka's distinctive qualities. The implication, obviously, is that Kafka read and was influenced by these precursors and tried to incorporate them into his work. However, as we move through this various and far-flung list, featuring authors from such vastly different times and places, we become increasingly doubtful whether Kafka would have read all of them. As we gradually realize, it is not that Kafka actually read these authors, or at least we could never conclusively prove this, but rather that Kafka operates as an excuse allowing his interpreter to put together this erudite and heterogeneous list. It is not that these authors have an obviously Kafkaesque quality or can be seen as naturally belonging together, but rather that in the light of Kafka's work we are now able to find some Kafka-like quality to them and a commonality between them. As Borges writes in the famous and much-quoted conclusion to his essay:

> The word 'precursor' is indispensable to the vocabulary of criticism, but one must try to purify it from any connotation of polemic or rivalry. The fact is that each writer *creates* his precursors. His work modifies our conception of the past, as it will modify the future. (*TL*, 365)

It is for this idea of a great writer creating their own precursors, influencing not only the future but also the past, that 'Kafka and His Precursors' is best remembered. It is this notion that is cited by such critics as Harold Bloom in *The Anxiety of Influence* and Gérard Genette in 'L'utopie littéraire', who extrapolate whole theories of literature from it.[4] But there is a much more profound and paradoxical notion that Borges outlines immediately before this that is rarely if ever taken up in readings of the essay. After running through the list of the precursors to Kafka's work, Borges concludes in an extraordinary statement:

> If I am not mistaken, the heterogeneous pieces I have listed resemble Kafka; if I am not mistaken, not all of them resemble each other. The last fact is what is most significant. Kafka's idiosyncrasy is present in each of these writings, to a greater or lesser degree, but if Kafka had not written, we would not perceive it; that is to say, it would not exist. (*TL*, 365)

What does Borges mean by this? How is it possible that all of the pieces Borges lists resemble Kafka and yet not all of them resemble each other? What exactly is going on here with Borges' exercise of literary comparison? Obviously, each of the authors Borges lists is an attempt to specify the peculiar quality that Kafka brings to literature. And, just as obviously, he lists a *number* of precursors because no single one of them is able to exhaust Kafka, to summarize what he represents. Indeed, we might even say that each new name added to the list is an attempt to supplement the ones before, to speak of some particular quality that the previous precursors did not encompass. It is this feeling that something has not yet been taken account of that allows us to keep on adding names to the list. In this sense, each new comparison represents a *failure* to define Kafka, a failure made clear by the one that comes after. Each successive entry on the list attempts to say what Kafka and the ones before have in common, what the *real* Kafka is that allowed those previous comparisons to be made. And the same goes even for the *first* comparison on the list. It too is not merely a comparison but already an attempt exhaustively to define Kafka, to speak of what it is about him that would allow any possible comparison.

But, as Borges makes clear when he speaks at the end of his essay of the way that 'the first Kafka of *Betrachtung* [the early short stories] is less a precursor of the Kafka of the gloomy myths and terrifying institutions than is Browning or Lord Dunsany' (*TL*, 365), any attempt to say what Kafka is is only to reduce him to one of his precursors. It is to see him as merely one of a potentially infinite series of qualities, thus allowing *another* to come along after and say what they all have in common. That is, what is missing in any comparison, and what each successive comparison tries to fill in, is the 'Kafka' that allows the comparison between these precursors and Kafka. Each new comparison draws out another quality of Kafka, and yet the Kafka that allows this comparison is always missing. This is the irony of all of those books of the form *Shakespeare and . . .* or *Joyce and . . .* or, indeed, *Borges and . . . .* They seek to put their finger on the unique and unreproducible quality of their chosen author; but they are able to do so only through a comparison with *another*, thus making them appear unoriginal, a lesser version of their precursors. In fact, pushing this argument to its furthest extent, it might be that it is the greatest of authors who inspire the most comparisons. It is they who of all authors can actually appear unoriginal, to add nothing to literature, to already be in all other authors.

However, for all of the sense that we miss the essence of Kafka in each comparison made with him, Kafka would also be nothing *outside of* these comparisons. The activity of the critic in finding sources or influences, of comparing a great author with others, is absolutely necessary. And even to attempt to avoid this by speaking of some real Kafka behind all of these comparisons is only to produce *another* comparison. Kafka does not exist outside of literary history, some expectation or preconception of how he should be read. In other words, in a paradox we have already seen, Kafka is at once outside of all comparison and only another in an endless series of comparisons. He is at the same time the incomparable Kafka that puts his precursors in a relationship with each other and, insofar as this Kafka must be named by some quality in order to be known at all, he is also what this Kafka and his precursors have in common. We might attempt to represent this diagrammatically:

'Kafka' $\Big\{$ $\dfrac{\text{Kafka}}{\text{Zeno Han Yu Kierkegaard Browning Bloy Dunsany}}$

To say what we see here: each precursor to Kafka does not merely add another quality to our conception of Kafka, but also attempts to say what all of those other qualities have in common. And yet, as we have seen, this itself opens up the possibility of another coming along and speaking of the 'Kafka' that this Kafka and all of those precursors have in common. What is revealed as the series of precursors goes on is that each attempt to summarize all of the previous predicates and say what they have in common becomes itself another in a potentially endless series of predicates, but this only from the perspective of a certain 'Kafka'. Importantly, we do not ever have a simple infinity or series of qualities with nothing in common. This series of qualities would be possible only insofar as they all stood in for a 'Kafka' that is the 'same'. Kafka, in the end, is neither an endless series of qualities with nothing in common (because this series would be possible only insofar as they all stood in for the same Kafka) nor what they all have in common (because he could only ever be grasped in terms of his always different precursors). Rather, 'Kafka' is the very *relationship between* these. 'Kafka' is what is in common to this series of predicates and that Kafka that appears to have nothing in common with them.

And if we go back to 'Kafka and His Precursors', we can see that it is this complex question of relationship that Kafka's work is already *about*. That is, if we look at the various authors Borges puts forward as possible precursors to Kafka, we find that in each there is raised this problem of something that is at once the same and different, incomparable and able to be grasped only through comparison. In Zeno, the distance from A to B is infinitely divisible, so that we can never get from one point to another; but this only because we are already at B, because in a sense we are counting back from B. In Han Yu, the unicorn is different from the horse, the bull, the wolf and the deer; but it can also only be compared to them, is made up only of parts taken from them. In Kierkegaard, the North Pole is at once everywhere and nowhere, can never be reached and is implicit in every journey. In Browning, the absence of God is God and His forgery proof of His existence. And in the final two examples, Borges provides two variants of Zeno's paradox: in Bloy, the travellers arrive at their destination without ever leaving; in Dunsany, they travel forever without arriving. In all of this, we can see that what the various texts cited have in common is not any literary style, thematic content or even a cultural or geographical locality, but a *logic*. It is the logic, we might say, of relationship. Precisely what Kafka, as seen through his precursors, can be seen to be introducing into literature is the question of relationship. And it is perhaps first of all the relationship between an author and their reader. This is why it is entirely appropriate that it is *Borges* in the end who is the 'Kafka' that Kafka and his precursors have in common. It is Borges who sees the relationship between Kafka and his various precursors, and thus makes of Kafka his own precursor. It is only Borges who has read this far-flung list, and who all of these authors, who would otherwise have nothing in common, can be seen to have in common.

### 'PIERRE MENARD, AUTHOR OF THE *QUIXOTE*'

'Pierre Menard, Author of the *Quixote*' is undoubtedly one of Borges' most famous and critically elaborated texts. It has had a major influence not only on the entire course of post-war literature, but also on art, philosophy, literary criticism and aesthetics. The story is an indispensable reference in a wide variety of intellectual fields and has itself gone through several waves of interpretation. It has been taken up within analytical philosophy as raising the question of what is a work of art and what is the role of the intention of the artist in making it.[5] It has been seen within the literary criticism of the 1960s and 1970s as pointing towards the anti-mimetic nature of the modernist work of art.[6] In the 1980s, it was read by structuralist and post-structuralist critics as demonstrating the intertextuality of works of art, the way works of art make their meaning by reference to other works.[7] More recently, post-colonial critics have argued that the story is an example of how to write in the 'frontier' spaces of provincial cultures, in which canonical texts must be re-imagined in local terms.[8] Finally, cutting against many of these readings, other critics have asserted the historical and referential nature of Borges' text, the way its real subject is the war that was being waged at the time it was written.[9] And, beyond its wide-ranging cultural effects, 'Pierre Menard' also has an intriguing 'autobiographical' dimension. The story originally appeared in *Sur* in May 1939, and is often claimed to be Borges' first. It is said in a well-known and often-repeated anecdote – first told by Borges himself – that it was written after Borges had spent several weeks in hospital hovering between life and death after contracting septicaemia, and that he wanted to see if he had recovered by trying to write something he had never written before: a short story. In fact, Borges had already written the story 'The Approach to Al-Mu'tasim'. It is even possible, according to some biographers, that Borges' accident only interrupted a writing of 'Pierre Menard' that was already underway.[10] But there is, nevertheless, something inaugural about 'Pierre Menard'. As many critics have pointed out, there is a certain identification made between Borges and the central character of his story. It is an identification based on a sense of mutual failure, for like Menard before his audacious literary experiment Borges too had lacked any central focus to his various literary endeavours. In realizing Menard, Borges realized himself; and in Menard's extraordinary experiment, Borges found a literary method that would serve him in a way until the end of his career.

'Pierre Menard' takes the form of a brief retrospective account of the work of the obscure twentieth-century French writer Pierre Menard. More exactly, the story sees itself as a correction or 'rectification' (*CF*, 88) of previous summaries, a defence of Menard against those who have deliberately set out to misrepresent him. As well as giving us some sense of the petty literary world from which Menard comes, it is important for the ultimate logic of the story that we are caught up from the outset in a certain correction of a correction. It is to begin to think hint at not only the underlying dialectical nature of the text, but more profoundly the whole idea of something standing in for its opposite. Our narrator, in seeking to set the record straight, starts with what he calls the 'visible' (*CF*, 88) production that was left behind after Menard's death. On the list are items dealing with subjects that Borges himself was interested in and on which he had already written: a study of the proposed solutions to Zeno's paradox; three monographs dealing with various aspects of *ars combinatoria* or the creation of texts through the systematic arrangement of letters or symbols; a poem rewriting one by the French symbolist Paul Valéry and an essay criticizing Valéry (which nevertheless represented the 'exact reverse' (*CF*, 90) of Menard's true opinion). Also listed amongst Menard's 'visible' work is a poem that appears twice with variants in the review *La Conque*; an article containing a suggestion for improving the game of chess by removing one of the rook's pawns, a suggestion the article ultimately retracts; a study of the poetic rules of French prose, and a defence of this study against a critic who says that no such rules exist; and a series of lines of poetry that owe their excellence to punctuation. What is most evident in this list is the emphasis on games (chess) and the ludic nature of language (the essays on combining words and the translation or transposition of existing texts to produce new ones). There is also the continuing theme of Menard being engaged in polemical argumentation, not only with others but also with himself (the defence against a critic of his study of the poetic rules of French prose; the putting forward and then withdrawal of his suggestion for improving chess).

The narrator then turns to what he calls, not a little grandiloquently, the 'subterranean', the 'interminably heroic' – which is to say, 'the 'unfinished' and invisible (*CF*, 90) – part of Menard's oeuvre: the literal rewriting without copying of two complete chapters and part of a chapter of the great Spanish writer Miguel de Cervantes' *Don Quixote*. Two texts, suggests the narrator, originally inspired Menard's undertaking. The first was a fragment by the German Romantic Novalis, in which he advocates the notion of a 'total identification' (*CF*, 90) with a particular author. The second, on the contrary, was one of those novels that sets a famous historical figure, like Christ or Hamlet or indeed Don Quixote, in a contemporary setting in order to produce the comedy of 'anachronism' or, worse, to remind us that all times and places are 'the same, or are different' (*CF*, 91). And Menard *does* at first attempt the task of a total identification with Cervantes. As the narrator puts it: 'Learn Spanish, return to Catholicism, fight against the Moor or Turk, forget the history of Europe from 1602 to 1918 – *be* Miguel de Cervantes' (*CF*, 91). However, ultimately rejecting the possibilities both of sameness and of difference, Menard in his undertaking decides rather to 'conjoin in a single figure . . . both the Ingenious Gentleman Don Quixote and his squire' (*CF*, 91). That is, analogously to this idea of putting together both Quixote and Sancho Panza, Menard seeks to come to the experience of Cervantes while still remaining himself. Again, as our narrator puts it: 'Being, somehow, Cervantes, and arriving thereby at the *Quixote* – that looked to Menard less challenging (and therefore less interesting) than continuing to be Pierre Menard and coming to the *Quixote through the experiences of Pierre Menard'* (*CF*, 91).

Later in the story, the narrator quotes from a letter Menard once sent to him, in which he outlines his method in more detail. Menard is guided in his attempt to recreate the book by a 'general recollection of the *Quixote*, simplified by forgetfulness and indifference', which might well be 'the equivalent of the vague foreshadowing of a yet unwritten book' (*CF*, 92). Thus in a first moment Menard improvizes, carried along by the 'inertiae of language and imagination' (*CF*, 92). Then – and here, once more, the theme of cancelling and correction that runs throughout the story – Menard gradually revises the excesses produced by that first moment in order to come closer to the 'original'. Finally, after many years of unremitting effort, Menard produces a word for word recreation of chapters 9 and 38 and a section of chapter 22 of the first part of *Don Quixote*. In one of the most important and often-cited passages not just in Borges but in all of contemporary literature, our narrator attempts to explain what Menard had achieved by comparing respective passages from Cervantes and Menard:

> The Cervantes text and the Menard text are verbally identical, but the second is almost infinitely richer. (More *ambiguous*, his detractors will say – but ambiguity is richness.)
>
> It is a revelation to compare the *Don Quixote* of Pierre Menard with that of Miguel de Cervantes. Cervantes, for example, wrote the following (Part I, chapter IX):
>
>> . . . truth, whose mother is history, rival of time, depository of deeds, witness of the past, exemplar and adviser to the present, and the future's counsellor.
>
> This catalogue of attributes, written in the seventeenth century, and written by the 'ingenious layman' Miguel de Cervantes, is

mere rhetorical praise of history. Menard, on the other hand, writes:

> ... truth, whose mother is history, rival of time, depository of deeds, witness of the past, exemplar and adviser to the present, and the future's counsellor.

History, the *mother* of truth! – the idea is staggering. Menard, a contemporary of William James, defines history not as a *delving into* reality but as the very *fount* of reality. Historical truth, for Menard, is not 'what happened'; it is what we *believe* happened. The final phrases – *exemplar and adviser to the present, and the future's counsellor* – are brazenly pragmatic.

The contrast in styles is equally striking. The archaic style of Menard – who is, in addition, not a native speaker of the language he writes – is somewhat affected. Not so the style of his precursor, who employs the Spanish of his time with complete naturalness. (*CF*, 94)

Our narrator then concludes his account with the thought that Menard in his undertaking potentially opens up an entirely new literary practice of 'deliberate anachronism' and 'fallacious attribution' (*CF*, 95). For example, he suggests that now, thanks to Menard, we might be able to read Homer's *Odyssey* as though it came after and not before the *Aeneid*. We might be able to read the fifteenth-century devotional text *Imitatio Christi* as though it were written by those religious and literary heretics James Joyce and Louis-Ferdinand Céline. We might even be able to read, suggests our narrator in an arch backhander, Madame Henri Bachelier's *Le jardin de centaure* as though it were written by Madame Henri Bachelier. (The great sin of Madame Bachelier appears to have been including in her list of Menard's work 'a literal translation of Quevedo's literal translation of St Francis de Sales' *Introduction à la vie dévote*' (*CF*, 90). Bachelier's inclusion perhaps earns the ire of the narrator insofar as it seems to pre-empt his own brilliant re-imagining of Menard's project of rewriting the *Quixote* and even his suggestion that a publicly scandalous writer – here, the seventeenth-century Spaniard Francisco de Quevedo – be understood as the author of a religious text.)

What is going on here in 'Pierre Menard'? How are we to understand the meaning of Menard's activity? In what sense can the narrator insist that Menard's version of the *Quixote* is 'almost infinitely richer' than Cervantes', even though the two versions are verbally identical? Of course, what the story plays on is the fact that we read the *Quixote* differently when we believe it is written by Menard because we bring to it all of the literary, social and historical background of the time in which he lived, as though the book were somehow a response to it. Thus, a sentence like 'truth, whose mother is history', which written at the time of Cervantes appears like a piece of empty rhetoric of no great consequence, can now appear as highly marked or significant: truth is not henceforth eternal and unchanging but is a product of history and can only be grasped in history. Equally, with regard to the two authors' literary styles, what in Cervantes appears natural and unaffected now appears in Menard as forced and unnatural. It is already to think that Cervantes' original itself can no longer be grasped directly but only as the rejection or negation of another option. In a sense, what Menard plays out or literalizes in rewriting Cervantes is the fact that the reader always brings to a book their own expectations and preconceptions. They imagine the book as if they were the author, as if they themselves had written it. As a result, even Cervantes himself can only be imagined as the first Menard. He does not write the only or definitive version of the *Quixote*, but only one particular version, as tied to its own time and place as any other. He himself can only be understood to proceed as though he were copying a 'general recollection of the *Quixote*, simplified by forgetfulness and indifference'. When he executes his various drafts, he too can only think that he is getting closer to a 'yet unwritten book' that already exists and awaits merely its realization.

To this extent, it is possible to argue that there is *no* true or authentic reading of a text. It is only ever the effect of its context, of the specific circumstances in which it is encountered. Every reading of the text implies a different text, so that what ends up being produced is a potentially infinite series of different versions with nothing in common between them. There is thus opened up in 'Pierre Menard' a certain relativism or even nihilism. It is certainly along these lines that the story is usually read and alternately praised for liberating interpretation from the canon or denounced for the loss of cultural standards. And yet we would argue that this is not properly to see what is at stake in the story. It is not to see that Menard's proposal to rewrite the *Quixote* is perhaps the 'exact reverse' of what he believes, or at least the relativist interpretation or the story is not entirely to exhaust its consequences. In order to show this, let us go back to that passage in which the narrator argues that Menard's version is 'almost infinitely richer' than Cervantes'. In fact, we can say that the two versions are different only insofar as they can be compared in some way. This is indeed why Borges on behalf of his narrator very carefully writes that Menard's version is only 'almost infinitely richer' [*casi infinitamente más rico*]: only '*almost* infinitely richer' because this difference is possible only on the basis that they are also the *same*. And a similar argument applies even if we displace the problem to the respective contexts in which the two versions are read. For all of the vast differences in context between the respective circumstances in which the *Quixote* is read by Cervantes and Menard, there must still be some context that they *do* share, from which their difference can be seen.

It is this that perhaps gets us towards the true logic of the story, one largely not seen by its legions of commentators. No reading of a text believes that it interprets it as it wants, sees in it merely a reflection of its own time and place. Indeed, every reading of a text – but let us take for a moment an 'academic' one that attempts to add something to the history of interpretation of it – is not only an attempt to speak of the text, but also an attempt to summarize and stand in for all previous attempts. However, as Menard reveals, even the most literal attempt to read a book, to speak of the real *Quixote* that lies behind all the others, is only to produce yet another reading, just as bound to its own particular time and place as any other. And yet, again, this itself could only be said from the perspective of *another Quixote* that would be what is in common to this reading and all of those others of which it speaks. In the end, exactly as with 'Kafka and His Precursors', what is revealed is that the '*Quixote*' is neither a series of particular readings nor some unchanging core of meaning, but the very *relationship between* these. The *Quixote* is at once something more transcendent than any mere 'foreshadowing' or memory of a book, for any attempt to realize it would produce only another copy, and only an endless series of different readings with nothing in common. It is for this reason that Menard makes the point that we cannot grasp the *Quixote* by simply becoming Cervantes, but only by 'continuing to be Pierre Menard and coming to the *Quixote* through the experiences of Pierre Menard', for the *Quixote* is the very inseparability of the original and the copy, truth and history, the writer and the reader. We might attempt to represent this diagrammatically:

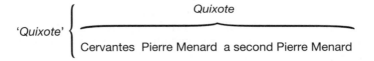

And, again, as with Kafka in 'Kafka and His Precursors', the choice of the Q*uixote* as the object of Menard's rewriting is not coincidental, for 'Pierre Menard' is in part about what makes a book a 'classic'. It is not, against the common humanist cliché, that it is some unchanging masterpiece that passes down eternal truths. It is rather the fact that it understands itself as always open to re-reading, that it exists from the beginning in a relationship with a reader with whom it may have nothing in common. It is along these lines that Borges interpreted the *Quixote* in the many essays he devoted to it throughout his career; and it explains his almost exclusive concentration on the famous prologue to part II of the novel, in which the characters, in a way like Scheherazade in *1001 Nights*, read the first part of the story they are in, thus confusing the boundary between the inside and the outside of the novel (*TL*, 160–161). Again, however, a great novel like the *Quixote* is not simply subject to this process of reading, but also tries to formulate its truth. What remains the lasting lesson of the *Quixote* is that the work of art is always open to the outside, is inevitably misread and misinterpreted by its audience. And that this applies first of all to itself, enunciating this 'truth'. But it is insofar as it understands itself therefore as empty, lacking all content, that a great novel lives on, proves itself to be, in Borges' word, 'immortal'. As Borges writes in one of his essays on the *Quixote*: 'The page that becomes immortal

can traverse the fire of typographical errors, approximate translations and inattentive or erroneous readings without losing its
soul in the process' (*TL*, 54). Certainly, one of the most striking
things about 'Pierre Menard' is that, against all of those readings of the story as an exercise in the 'death of the author' or the
relativity of meaning, Borges precisely tries to find a formal or
fictional equivalent in his story to what he sees as the novel's true
message.

## 'THE LIBRARY OF BABEL'

'The Library of Babel' is another of Borges' signature stories,
endlessly quoted and referred to, a veritable emblem of our time.
Originally published in *The Garden of Forking Paths*, it was one
of the two Borges stories translated into French by Néstor Ibarra
for the wartime *Les Lettres françaises* that began the slow process of making Borges' reputation overseas. Said to have been
inspired by Borges' time as a shelver of books at the Miguel
Cané Municipal Library, the story was written during a difficult
period of Borges' life. Many years later in an interview with
Georges Charbonnier, Borges was to describe it as arising out of
'a feeling of loneliness, of anguish, of uselessness, of the mysterious nature of the universe, of time, and, what is most important,
ourselves'.[11] And this diagnosis has been echoed by the story's
interpreters, who have largely over the years seen the story
as either about the futility of searching for meaning in an indifferent universe or a metaphor for the decline or exhaustion of
Western culture.[12] Today, however, its vision of the possibility
of the total availability of all knowledge is viewed in a more
optimistic mode, thanks to the advent of the computer and the
internet, and there is now a whole literature devoted to the connections between Borges' story and contemporary information
technologies.[13] There are as well a number of recent publications
exploring the relationship between 'The Library of Babel' and
mathematics, particularly post-Cantorian set theory.[14] But, as so
often with Borges, interpreters often leap to analogies or seek to
make comparisons to other fields of knowledge without first
reading the story closely. To understand properly what Borges
has added to the questions of the search for human meaning, the
exhaustion of literature and the new information technologies,

it is first necessary to understand what the story is saying in its own terms.

'The Library of Babel' begins with an extraordinary *visual* image, a superb and justly celebrated description of a Library that stretches away before our eyes towards a far distant horizon. It is a description that was perhaps influenced by a picture of a labyrinth Borges saw as a young boy, a depiction of a lonely Minotaur trapped inside a maze by the nineteenth-century English painter George Watts, and the prison etchings of Piranesi, as described by Thomas De Quincey. It is a description that might remind more contemporary readers of the strange topologies of M. C. Escher and the computer-generated spectacles of such films as *The Matrix*. Borges' description – and this is what is so effective about it – is at once sublime in its scale and domestic in its details, a vision of seemingly infinitely replicated galleries and connecting staircases hanging mysteriously in mid-air and of the unbearably cloistered and confined spaces of the Librarians who inhabit this world. Borges writes:

The universe (which others call the Library) is composed of an indefinite, perhaps infinite number of hexagonal galleries. In the centre of each gallery is a ventilation shaft, bounded by a low railing. From any hexagon one can see the floors above and below – one after another, endlessly. The arrangement of the galleries is always the same. Twenty bookshelves, five to each side, line four of the hexagon's six sides; the height of the bookshelves, floor to ceiling, is hardly greater than the height of a normal librarian. One of the hexagon's free sides opens onto a narrow sort of vestibule, which in turn opens onto another gallery, identical to the first – identical in fact to all. To the left and right of the vestibule are two tiny compartments. One is for sleeping, upright; the other, for satisfying one's physical necessities. Through this space, too, there passes a spiral staircase, which winds upward and downward to the remotest distance. In the vestibule there is a mirror, which faithfully duplicates appearances. Men often infer from this mirror that the Library is not infinite – if it were, what need would there be for that illusory replication? I prefer to dream that the burnished surfaces are a figuration and promise of the infinite . . . (*CF*, 112)

What is this 'perhaps infinite' [*tal vez infinito*] Library made up of? It is here that we see one of Borges' long-running fascinations, already given ironic expression in the list of Menard's 'visible' productions. It is the idea of the systematic permutation of a limited number of symbols, whether alphabetic or otherwise, to produce a potentially unlimited number of outcomes. This possibility can be seen, for example, in Borges' essay on Raymón Llull's 'thinking machine', which by the different arrangements of a series of discs on which various symbols are printed produces an enormous number of prophesies and predictions (*TL*, 155–159). Or it can be seen in Borges' important essay 'The Doctrine of Cycles', in which he considers the notion that all things in the universe will eventually repeat themselves because the number of possible combinations of atoms will one day run out (*TL*, 115–122). Indeed, in August 1939, just a few months before he wrote 'The Library of Babel', Borges published the essay 'The Total Library' in *Sur*, in which he sketched the history of the imagining of a total library that would contain all possible books through the endless variation of all the letters in the alphabet (*TL*, 214–216). In 'The Library of Babel' itself, it is stated that its books are made up of every possible combination of the twenty-five orthographical symbols – twenty-two letters, the comma, the full stop and the space – within the format of books of 410 pages, with 40 lines per page, approximately 80 letters per line and a title on its cover. These permutations continue endlessly, so that, as a 'librarian of genius' (*CF*, 114) once noted, there are no two identical books in all of the Library. As the narrator goes on to elaborate:

> The Library is 'total' – perfect, complete and whole – and its bookshelves contain all possible combinations of the twenty-two orthographical symbols (a number which, though unimaginably vast, is not infinite) – that is, all that is able to be expressed, in every language. *All* – the detailed history of the future, the autobiographies of the archangels, the faithful catalogue of the Library, thousands and thousands of false catalogues, the proof of the falsity of those false catalogues, a proof of the falsity of the *true* catalogue, the Gnostic gospel of Basilides, the commentary upon that gospel, the commentary on the commentary on that gospel, the true story of your

death, the translation of every book into every language, the interpolations of every book into all books. (*CF*, 115)

It is this that leads to the consideration of the great question that exercises the librarians of the Library of Babel. After concluding that the books within the Library are made up of all the possible combinations of the twenty-five orthographical symbols and that no two books are identical, they are then faced with the problem of how the Library can be 'infinite', as it is said to be. For they realize that, expressed in these terms, the Library is *not* actually infinite. Mathematicians have calculated that, using the parameters Borges sets out, the number of books in the Library would be $25^{1,312,000}$, more than the number of atoms in the universe, but still not infinite. Nevertheless, despite this, the narrator is still able to assert that the Library is infinite. How is this so? He provides his answer in the final words of the story, in terms that might remind us of the philosopher Immanuel Kant's cosmological antinomy in his *Critique of Pure Reason*, in which he rejects the possibility both that the world does come to an end and that it does not come to an end:

> I have just written the word 'infinite'. I have not included that adjective out of mere rhetorical habit; I hereby state that it is not illogical to think that the world is infinite. Those who believe it to have limits hypothesize that in some remote place or places the corridors and staircases and hexagons may, inconceivably, end – which is absurd. And yet those who picture the world as unlimited forget that the number of books is *not*. I will be bold enough to suggest this solution to the ancient problem: *The Library is unlimited but periodic.* If an eternal traveller should journey in any direction, he would find after untold centuries that the same volumes are repeated in the same disorder – which, repeated, becomes order: the Order. (*CF*, 118)

So how is it that the Library can be infinite if it is not in fact infinite? Or, better, how to think the Library as *both* finite and infinite? And how, finally, might all this relate to that logic of the labyrinth we have previously seen in other of Borges' stories? How, in other words, might we find the 'Borgesian' in

'The Library of Babel', which as we have argued is not a matter of any particular writerly style or narrative theme, but more a matter of *logic*? We might begin here with a moment from the previous passage we cited, in which the narrator speaks of the way that, given that the Library contains 'all that is able to be expressed', within the Library there is not only the faithful catalogue of the Library and thousands and thousands of false catalogues, but also the proof of the falsity of those false catalogues and even the proof of the falsity of the true catalogue. Of course, when we read this, what is raised is the very truth of *this* statement itself, insofar as it would be subject to the rule of possible refutation it enunciates. In other words, as many commentators have pointed out, there is no simple objective statement possible about the Library because this statement would itself be subject to the rule of the Library. And yet, equally, this could not be said, even this would not be true, unless there *were* something of this statement outside of the Library, not subject to its rule. In a sense, that is, the fact that there is nothing outside of the Library, that everything is subject to its rule, would be possible only because there *is* something outside of the Library – but the effect of this is to make this outside appear inside the Library and subject once more to its rule of refutation. No truth about the Library is ever simply true, but only stands in for its opposite and refutation, is, as it were, a refutation of its refutation.

We might put all of this another way. The narrator elsewhere speaks of the 'superstition' that there must exist somewhere in the Library a true catalogue of the rest of the Library, 'a book that is the cipher and perfect compendium *of all other books*' (*CF*, 116). The librarian who has read this catalogue, it is reasoned, must in some way be analogous to a God. But then the question is asked: how to find this catalogue? At first a method proceeding via regression is proposed. As the narrator describes it: 'To first locate book A, first consult book B, which tells us where book A can be found; to locate book B, first consult book C, and so on, to infinity . . .' (*CF*, 117) What is being hinted at here, what produces this infinite regress, is the fact that this catalogue, despite being the catalogue of 'all other books', is itself inside the Library. There is necessarily implied, therefore, *another* catalogue that would catalogue both this catalogue *and* the Library it catalogues. And this catalogue would in turn require another to catalogue *it*, and so on. It is this that produces that infinite regress, in which we move from catalogue A to catalogue B to catalogue C. Indeed, within one of the almost infinitely many languages of the Library, *every* book could be this catalogue, every book in the Library attempts to speak about the Library, about 'all other books' in the Library. And, of course, it is for just this reason that *no* book can be the definitive catalogue of the Library, for it could no sooner be nominated as such than there would be required *another* that catalogues it. In this sense, the catalogue would be not so much some actual book as at once all books and no books. The idea of the catalogue *doubles* the Library, not so much imposing an order as repeating its disorder.

And, in fact, when we look at 'The Library of Babel', any number of objects play the role of this catalogue. To begin with, the story itself that we read is a kind of 'catalogue' of the Library, at once an attempt to clarify, abstract, state from the outside its rules and only a potentially meaningless series of orthographical symbols, subject to its rule. In a similar position too are the librarians, who likewise are outside of the Library, rationally attempting to formulate its rules, and inside the Library, subject to the normal human dogmas and superstitions, incapable of more than guessing at the Library's true principles. But perhaps the most revealing analogue to or translation of the catalogue are those mirrors in the Library's vestibules, which as the narrator says are a 'figuration and promise' of the infinite. For, of course, a mirror is a 'catalogue' of the Library, an attempt to capture it, reflect it, reflect upon it from somewhere else. But if we can draw out what is implied here a little more, how would it be possible to represent or reflect upon a literally infinite object? What distance would a mirror have to be from it in order to capture it on its surface? If we think of something like a telescope, an infinite distance – or, to put it another way, it would be *impossible* to reflect like a mirror a literally infinite object. Nevertheless, we would also say that it is only reflected in a mirror that the Library would be infinite. Its infinity would not exist until it had been represented in some way. What is this ultimately to suggest? If the Library necessarily includes its catalogue because it contains 'all that is able to be expressed', but contains 'all that is able to be expressed' only because of its catalogue, where is infinity to be found here? As we have seen in all of the Borges stories we have looked at so far, it exists in the very *relationship between* the Library and its catalogue. Every attempt to speak of the Library from the outside is revealed to be inside the Library, but this in turn only because of another position outside of the Library. We might attempt to represent this diagrammatically:

$$\text{'catalogue'} \left\{ \begin{array}{c} \overbrace{\text{catalogue}} \\ \text{Library} \end{array} \right.$$

All of this might be expressed in still another way, for we might ask how is it that the Library is infinite and able to express 'all that is able to be expressed' when we know that the actual number of books comes to an end? The clue lies in that passage where the narrator speak of the way that 'some have suggested that each letter influences the next, and that the value of MCV on page 71, line 3, is not the value of the same series of letters on another line of another page' (*CF*, 114), for this is to remind us of 'Pierre Menard', in which the repetition of the same letter in different circumstances produces a different meaning. It is ultimately to speak of the way that we can permute not merely letters but also books, read the books in the Library not in any single, linear order, but in a kind of wandering in which we encounter them in any order. In this sense, there would be as many Libraries as there are paths through the Library, with each different route allowing us to read its books differently. We can even imagine us moving not merely between different books but different *parts* of books, thus increasing exponentially again the number of possible Libraries. But, nevertheless, so long as we move through the Library in a single unbroken line, reading each book or part of a book just once, the Library will always come to an end. What is truly required for an infinite Library is the possibility of *repeating* oneself, of reading the same book *twice*. And this itself repeatedly. In other words, between any two points of the Library it must be possible to insert the rest of the Library, and within this Library insert the rest of the Library, and so on.

We would never actually have infinity, but the coming to the end of the Library can be indefinitely deferred. And yet – this again is our point about infinity existing only within limits – all of this only because we can repeat; this indefinite deferral is only a kind of counting back from the end. We have not an actual infinity, but rather endless 'interpolations' [*las interpolaciones*: crucially plural] between two, an infinity of *always one more*.

To conclude here: what exactly *is* the Library of Babel? It is – and this is why the last of those twenty-five orthographical symbols is the most important – the *space between* things. We see this, to begin, with the notion of refutation in the Library. As we have seen, not only does the fact that something is in the Library render it liable to be refuted, but this refutation itself is always able to be refuted. The process of refutation never stops or is never able to be grasped as such, but permanently divides things from themselves, meaning that something exists only as the negation of its negation, as standing in for its possible absence or opposition. And we see the same thing with the idea of a catalogue to the Library. Again, the catalogue is not so much some actual book as a process or hypothesis that permanently divides the Library from itself. Now even the same book in the Library is both the catalogue of 'all other books' and merely one of 'all other books'. Finally, as we saw with the reading of the books within the Library, the Library must be understood as what comes between any two points of the Library, and this itself indefinitely. It is both the infinite space that opens up within the same letter or book and what attempts to stand in for that space. In each case here, the Library is total, but only because of a certain space outside of it. It is precisely for this reason that it is never a matter, insofar as the Library is a labyrinth, of only one labyrinth but always two, a labyrinth inside a labyrinth: the labyrinth of Ts'ui Pen inside the labyrinth of Albert's garden; the labyrinth of the City of Immortals inside the labyrinth of underground passages; the labyrinth of the catalogue inside the labyrinth of the Library. It is to suggest that the labyrinth is always split between an inside and an outside; that it can only ever be infinite insofar as it has an outside, but that this outside in turn can only ever be understood as being inside. The split between the labyrinth and the world is also always a choice between two paths in the labyrinth. There is only the labyrinth, but only insofar as we cannot be sure whether we are inside of it or not, whether indeed it exists or not.

## STUDY QUESTION 1

Borges, as we have seen, has written essays and stories on both Zeno's paradox and the paradoxes of self-referentiality. But how do these seemingly different fields of intellectual enquiry come together in his work? We might note that the problem of finding the catalogue of the Library of Babel (*CF*, 117) is an example both of Zeno's paradox and of logical infinite regression. We might also note that in *Otras inquisiciones* Borges puts together the essays 'Kafka and His Precursors', on problems of self-referentiality, and 'Avatars of the Tortoise', on Zeno's paradox. Is Zeno's paradox the same as the problem of self-referentiality for Borges? Is this to point to some overall logic to his work, which crosses the fields of logic and mathematics?

## STUDY QUESTION 2

We have commented on the way that Borges uses the qualification 'almost infinitely richer [*casi infinitamente más rico*]' (*CF*, 94, *OC* I, 449) to comment on Menard's version of *Don Quixote* in relation to Cervantes'. We see a similar qualification at the beginning of 'The Library of Babel', where Borges speaks of a 'perhaps infinite number [*tal vez infinito*]' (*CF*, 112, *OC* I, 465) of hexagonal galleries. Why these qualifications, especially when the notion of the infinite appears to be involved? Where else can we see Borges using such qualifications of the infinite in his work?

## CHAPTER 4

# READING THE SHORT STORIES: INFINITY AND ONE

There have been many attempts to speak not just of the literary qualities of Borges' stories but also of their intellectual substance. From the beginning, Borges has been read as a writer who addresses a whole range of issues from the history of philosophy, to which he gives fictional expression. For example, the story 'Emma Zunz' is about the integrity of the human personality, 'The Writing of the God' is about the relationship of language to reality and 'The Other Death' is about the effect of time upon memory. More than this, specific philosophers and philosophical systems are either directly or indirectly referenced throughout Borges' work. We might think of the twelfth-century Islamic philosopher Ibn Rushd, who is a character in 'Averröes' Search', the Kabbalistic text *Sefer Yetsirah* or *Book of Creation* that is featured in 'The Secret Miracle' and the twentieth-century Italian philosopher Benedetto Croce, who writes the book that is at the centre of 'The Story of the Warrior and the Captive Maiden'. As well, Borges read and reviewed voluminously across several languages, not just stories and novels, but books on theology, sociology, mathematics and philosophy. He wrote a prologue for William James' *Varieties of Religious Experience* and reviewed James George Frazer's *The Fear of the Dead in Primitive Religion*. He wrote a capsule biography of Oswald Spengler and a prologue to Thorstein Veblen's *The Theory of the Leisure Class*. He wrote an essay based on Georg Cantor's theory of transfinite numbers and a review of Edward Kasner and James Newman's *Mathematics and the Imagination*. He wrote a prologue to Kierkegaard's *Fear and Trembling* and a review of Alfred North Whitehead's *Modes of Thought*.

As a result, when critics come to Borges' fiction they have almost *too many* philosophical references available to them. Not only do Borges' stories reference a vast array of philosophical sources that are not always consistent with each other, but it must furthermore be decided which of these references are essential and which are there only to form part of the background detail. Certainly, in the literature there is a wide divergence of opinion as to which philosophers or philosophical systems are truly influential on Borges' way of thinking. We might just offer here a brief overview of the way Borges has been taken up within philosophy, along with the names of the chief critics associated with the various interpretive viewpoints. Undoubtedly, the dominant reading of Borges has been as a philosophical idealist.[1] This is seen as committing him to a belief not only in the fundamental unreality of the world but also in the corresponding reality of mental or imagined objects. This is, of course, an entirely suitable doctrine for a novelist, whose business it is to create fictional universes that others can share; but Borges is also seen to be thoroughly aware of the philosophical tradition idealism comes out of: Plato, Berkeley, Kant, Schopenhauer. In a number of readings of Borges, the unreality of this earthly world is contrasted to the reality of a higher, spiritual one, which serves as its origin or explanation. Critics in this regard have read Borges variously in terms of his relationship to the Jewish Kabbalah, Eastern Buddhism or Western varieties of Gnosticism, Neo-Platonism and pantheism.[2] This spiritual reading of Borges has been widened to understand him in terms of a more general 'esoteric' tradition, which is the notion that behind appearances there is some hidden truth to the world that is available only to initiates through the reading of certain mystical texts.[3] This in turn leads to an emphasis on the role of language in Borges, either in terms of the ability language has to mirror or reflect a higher reality, as in the Jewish practice of 'midrash', or in terms of the capacity of language to separate us from reality, as in the sceptical argument that humans can never know the truth of the world.[4] Finally, something of this alternative can be seen in the long-running philosophical debate that takes place in Borges' work between realism and nominalism.[5] Realism, associated with such thinkers as Plato, argues for the actual existence of those categories like 'bed' and 'whiteness' that allow us to group together otherwise disparate objects. Nominalism, associated with such thinkers as John Stuart Mill, argues that these categories are mere heuristic devices, with no external or objective reality but only projections of the human mind in its desire to make meaning of the world.

Is it possible to generalize here and find some element in common to all of those linguistic, religious and philosophical systems that seem to be at stake in Borges' work? In fact, we would argue that idealism is *not* the conceptual centre of Borges' universe. As Borges often insists in interviews, his idealism is not to be taken straight, but operates instead as a point of departure for his fictions.[6] In that kind of argument against oneself that we have already seen, if Borges puts idealism forward in his work it is only ultimately to point towards its opposite, to show that it would not be possible without its corresponding materialism. This is Borges' difference from those traditions of Gnosticism, Neo-Platonism and the Kabbalah with which he is often associated. He denies even the possibility of us ever contacting this higher principle. His idealism is never to be seen as such, but only in the always material forms it takes in our world. If we read Borges' well-known essay 'Coleridge's Flower' (*TL*, 240–242) carefully, for example, we can see that, if this flower does embody the whole world, coming at the end of an infinite series of causes and effects, it can also only be grasped *within* the world, played out in another infinite series of causes and effects. It is this that in turn can lead to a criticism that places emphasis on the themes of scepticism and the failure of enlightenment in Borges' work, as though any aspiration to a higher principle were merely an illusion. But here again Borges is not simply to be identified with materialism. If we are never actually able to look behind appearances, these appearances themselves would not be possible without something else. It is this inseparability of idealism and materialism, realism and nominalism, let us say, the one and the infinite, that is the real logic behind Borges' work. We seek to trace this paradoxical identity of opposites through a close reading of three of Borges' stories here: 'The Zahir', 'The Aleph' and 'Funes, His Memory'.

## 'THE ZAHIR'

'The Zahir' is undoubtedly one of Borges' major stories, and one that has been read as a striking expression of many of his lasting philosophical preoccupations. It was originally published in the small review of which Borges was the editor,

*Los anales de Buenos Aires*, on July 17 1947. 'The Zahir' was to be the last of the pieces Borges was to write for *Los anales* (we have already seen him publish 'The Immortal' there), because a few weeks after 'The Zahir' came out Borges had a disagreement with the proprietor and resigned. After the story's initial appearance, it was included in the collection *El Aleph*. In fact, 'The Zahir' was the second of Borges' stories to be translated into English (after 'The Garden of Forking Paths' in 1948). It was published, in a translation by Dudley Fitts, in *Partisan Review* in February 1950, and was subsequently included in the famous 1962 collection *Labyrinths*, which made Borges' name in the English-speaking world. 'The Zahir' comes from that period of Borges' career when he was moving away from the 'essay-fictions' of *Ficciones* and towards more conventional short stories that featured, if not exactly psychologically well-rounded characters, at least deeply felt and imagined settings, with the mention of specific Buenos Aires suburbs and street names adding an extra touch of verisimilitude. But for all of this, critics can occasionally remain unconvinced by the sense of slowly mounting unease Borges tries to create in the story, something he attempts to do through a fabricated Islamic myth or legend involving a literally unforgettable object called a 'Zahir'. For example, Borges commentator Gene H. Bell-Villada, after speaking of the story's 'perfervid Oriental fantasia on Islamic themes', concludes his analysis with the following harsh assessment: "The Zahir' takes up a worthy idea – individual despair in the modern city. Unfortunately, Borges overburdens his text and thickens his prose with so many bookish ingredients that they obscure the story's central action'.[7]

Ironically, for all of this accusation of the story's bookishness and impersonality, 'The Zahir' is amongst Borges' most heartfelt and directly autobiographical pieces of writing. In its evocation of lost love or of love given without reciprocation, the story was inspired by Estela Canto, one of Borges' two great unrequited loves, who had left him the year before. 'The Zahir', indeed, begins with our narrator, Borges, attending the wake of a woman, one Teodelina Villar, with whom he had once been – and evidently still is – in love. Teodelina is described as a glamorous society woman, the photographs of whom were once featured 'ubiquitously' in the pages of 'worldly magazines' (*CF*, 242). She was a fanatical follower all the way from distant Buenos Aires of the latest French styles, which would no sooner arrive than they would 'almost immediately pass out of fashion' (*CF*, 243). As a result of her desperate attempts to keep up, Teodelina passed through 'endless metamorphoses, as though fleeing from herself' (*CF*, 243). It is as though she sought, as Borges puts it, not merely the 'absolute', but the 'absolute in the ephemeral' (*CF*, 243). At her wake, Teodelina as she lies in repose seems almost magically to recover her previous self, the one with whom Borges originally fell in love. Moved by her death, but unable to admit it to himself, he deliberately seeks to break the spell, and after leaving the gathering of Teodelina's friends and relatives in the hours of the early morning he calls in at a neighbourhood bar that is still open. He orders a drink, and in his change receives a Zahir, an ordinary 20-centavo coin, into which is scratched the letters NT and the number 2.

Without paying it at the time any attention, Borges as he walks home after leaving the bar begins a series of musings on the various coins that are to be found throughout history and fiction:

> The thought struck me that there is no coin that is not the symbol of all the coins that shine endlessly down throughout history and fable. I thought of Charon's obolus; the alms that Belisarius went about begging for; Judas' thirty pieces of silver; the drachmas of the courtesan Laïs; the ancient coin proffered by one of the Ephesian sleepers; the bright coins of the wizard in the *1001 Nights*, which turned into disks of paper; Isaac Laquedem's inexhaustible denarius; the sixty thousand coins, one for every line of an epic, which Firdusi returned to a king because they were silver and not gold; the gold doubloon nailed by Ahab to the mast; Leopold Bloom's unreturning florin; the gold louis that betrayed the fleeing Louis XVI near Varennes. (*CF*, 244)

After wandering around in a circle and becoming lost, Borges then decides to take a cab home. While on his way, he further ponders:

> I reflected that there is nothing less material than money, since any coin (a twenty-centavo piece, for instance) is, in truth, a panoply of possible futures. *Money is abstract*, I said

over and over, *money is future time*. It can be an evening just
outside the city, or a Brahms melody, or maps, or chess, or
coffee, or the words of Epictetus, which teach contempt of
gold; it is a Proteus more changeable than the Proteus of the
isle of Pharos. (*CF*, 244–245)

Home at last, he falls asleep, and has a dream in which he is 'a
pile of coins guarded by a gryphon' (*CF*, 245).

The next day, Borges awakes, decides that he must have been
drunk and determines to get rid of the coin. He goes to another
bar, deliberately taking care not to remember its address, and
buys a drink using his Zahir. Until the end of the month, he dis-
tracts himself by writing a tale of fantasy, which is told from
the point of view of a serpent guarding some treasure against
those who would come to steal it. After successfully completing
the story, he is so confident he has forgotten the Zahir that
on a number of occasions he deliberately recalls it to mind.
However, as he is later to remark ruefully: 'The truth is, I abused
these moments; starting to recall turned out to be much easier
than stopping' (*CF*, 246). He is henceforth unable to forget
the Zahir, unable as it were, *not* to recall it. He attempts to
dislodge the thought of the actual Zahir by substituting for it
other coins – a Chilean 5- and 10-centavo piece, an Uruguayan
2-centavo piece, a British pound – but these attempts fail, and he
soon finds himself back thinking of the Zahir. In despair, Borges
decides to consult a psychiatrist. He is unable to admit to them
the exact form of the obsession from which he suffers and
describes it only in general form. He is unable to free his mind,
he tells them, from a 'random object, a coin, say' (*CF*, 246).
A little while later, while browsing a bookshop, Borges comes
across a copy of Julius Barlach's *Urkunden zur Geschichte der
Zahirsage* [*Documents Relating to the Thinking of the Legend of
the Zahir*]. It reveals to him for the first time the exact condition
from which he is suffering and the fact that he is not the first to
have suffered it. Barlach speaks of something called a 'Zahir',
derived from the Arabic word for 'visible', and referring in
Muslim countries to 'beings or things which have the terrible
power to be unforgettable, and whose image eventually drives
people mad' (*CF*, 246). It has variously been throughout history
a copper astrolabe, a tiger, an idol called Yahuk and a prophet

from Khorasan who wore a veil. Barlach furthermore goes on to say that, although there is 'no creature in the world that did not tend to toward becoming a *Zaheer*', God in His Mercy 'does not allow two beings to be a *Zaheer* at the same time' (*CF*, 247).

Borges, after reading Barlach's account, comes to realize the fate that is in store for him (and the events of the story are related in retrospect, while he is still able to narrate what happened to him). In fact, at Teodelina's wake, he had been surprised not to see her younger sister Julia. He soon discovers her unhappy circumstances, which are soon to be his own. 'Poor Julita', one of her friends tells him. 'She's become so odd. She's been put into Bosch. How she must be crushed by those nurses spoon-feeding her! She's still going on and on about the coin, just like Morena Sackmann's chauffeur' (*CF*, 248). Borges then makes the following grim prediction:

> Before the year 1948 [the story is said to be written in November], Julia's fate will have overtaken me. I will have to be fed and dressed, I will not know whether it's morning or night, I will not know who Borges was. (*CF*, 248)

However, as he then goes on to say, 'calling that future terrible is a fallacy, since none of the future's circumstances will in any way affect me. One might as well call 'terrible' the pain of an anesthetized patient whose skull is being trepanned' (*CF*, 248). Indeed, he goes on to conclude, in the final lines of the story, that he should – along the lines of certain religious devotees – even force himself to repeat the name of the Zahir precisely as a way of forgetting it. As he writes:

> In order to lose themselves in God, the Sufis repeat their own name or the ninety-nine names of God until the names mean nothing anymore. I long to travel that path. Perhaps by thinking about the Zahir unceasingly, I can manage to wear it away; perhaps behind the coin is God. (*CF*, 249)

What exactly is going on in 'The Zahir', and why is Borges able to conclude on this surprisingly positive note? Obviously, what is being related is the story of an obsession, as a result of which the narrator will be able to think only of the Zahir. It is a fate, once initial contact with the Zahir has been made, that is inevitable, that nothing can prevent. And yet, as Borges notes, when this obsession has entirely taken its course and he is unable to think of anything else, he would no longer be obsessed, or at least no longer know that he was obsessed. In other words, the same narration that tells the story of the Zahir also means that it has not yet taken place. As long as the narrator is able to relate the story of his obsession with the Zahir, he is not yet completely under its spell. We have here, of course – in common with a number of other Borges stories we have looked at – the same narrative structure as *1001 Nights*, in which Scheherazade endlessly postpones her fate by speaking about it. In 'The Zahir', the same story that Borges writes under the spell of the Zahir, and that in a way even *is* the Zahir, is also our only defence against it. And it is this that explains the final words of the story. It is not, as is commonly thought, a matter of endlessly chanting the name of the Zahir as a way of *losing* ourselves within it. Rather, it is a matter of *preserving* ourselves in the face of its overwhelming presence. As long as we can name the Zahir, we can know that we are not the Zahir, that we have not yet reached the terminal stage of its obsession, in which we are no longer aware of it because we cannot compare it to anything else.

We might put this another way. Throughout the story, a number of different objects are spoken of as having once been the Zahir. Borges is obsessed by a coin. Barlach's anthology lists a copper astrolabe, a tiger, an idol called Yahuk and a prophet from Khorasan. Earlier in the story, Borges himself mentions, as well as the astrolabe and the tiger, a sailor's compass, a vein of marble in a synagogue in Córdoba and the bottom of a well in a ghetto in Tetúan. It is with the *image* of these things that people become obsessed, unable to think of anything else. And yet, exactly insofar as the Zahir is visible, something with which we can become obsessed, we can know that this is not the real Zahir but only something that stands in for it, because the 'Zahir' properly speaking is what all of these objects are but is not strictly to be identified with any of them. It is undoubtedly for this reason that Barlach quotes in his text a line inserted into Farid al-Din Attär's *Asrar Nama* (*The Book of Things Unknown*) that says 'the Zahir is the shadow of the Rose and the rending of the veil', and writes that the one 'who has seen the Zahir soon shall see the Rose'. It is to indicate the way that behind each visible Zahir lies another, and that behind even this 'Zahir' lies the 'Rose'. What the story seems to be speaking of – it is this that leads to the reading of Borges' work in terms of various 'esoteric' doctrines – is some divine or mystical principle that secretly orders the world. In a manner akin to negative theology, it points to some hidden explanation of all that is, which everything else stands in for, like that all-encompassing flower of Coleridge.

Certainly, within this reading, Borges' love for Teodelina – of course, the real Zahir of the story – makes sense. For when she becomes 'what she had been twenty years before' (*CF*, 243) on the night of her wake, it is as though what is revealed to the narrator is an ideal or archetypal Teodelina, outside of the changes imposed by fashion. And this essentially platonic reading of the story has been put forward by a number of critics.[8] And yet what they overlook is that, even if he does not admit it, part of what fascinates Borges about Teodelina *is* her very snobbery and endless transformations, the surprising fact that for such a beautiful woman she always seemed to be 'fleeing from herself'. And the same goes for the Zahir itself. If in one way we can say that, insofar as we are obsessed by the Zahir, it cannot be the real Zahir, in another way the Zahir *is* defined by our being obsessed by it. As Barlach emphasizes, even though any actual Zahir only stands in for the real 'Zahir', there always is an actual Zahir. Indeed, what the history of the Zahir shows us is that a series of extremely ordinary objects have been the Zahir, that the objects that have successively played the role of the Zahir are just as arbitrary and contingent as Teodelina's fashions. Far from being some transcendent object that cannot be thought or represented, the Zahir just *is* that series of objects with no particular value or meaning of their own and that themselves always seem to be pointing elsewhere or exist only in relation to another (astrolabe, compass, idol, prophet, synagogue). This is why it is appropriate that the Zahir is represented by a *coin* in Borges' case, for money is at once the most precious object of all, that to which all else is compared, and in itself of no value at all, only the empty medium through which other objects are exchanged. The Zahir, that is, is at once higher than any representation of it and only an endless series of objects with nothing in common. It is the *relationship between* the Zahir for which all else stands in and those objects that stand in for it. We might attempt to represent this diagrammatically:

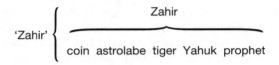

It is at this point that we return to the question of the one and the many that we say lies at the basis of Borges' work. As we have seen, critics are split over the question of whether Borges argues for an underlying principle to the world or for the sceptical conclusion that this principle is forever to be denied to us. But we go further than this, which can be understood to imply that this principle still exists somewhere, even if inaccessible to humans. We argue that, if we could not even remark upon the heterogeneity or infinite difference of the world without some category that everything has in common, this category itself would only ever exist in always different forms. There is *nowhere* – and here lies Borges' difference from all varieties of Platonism or religion – where it exists before entering the world. What then is the status of this ordering principle, if it can never actually be realized? We say that it operates exactly like the Zahir in Borges' story. To think it is *not* to think it. Ironically, it is when the narrator 'willfully remembers it' (*CF*, 246) that it is not the Zahir, insofar as the Zahir is defined as what in its complete state we are unaware of. And yet it is also when we do *not* think of the Zahir that we think of it. As the narrator realizes as a result of his exercise in deliberate recall, in an example of that double negation we have seen throughout Borges, not to think of the Zahir must be understood as an effort precisely *not* to think of it. And the same contradiction can be seen earlier with regard to the Stoic philosopher Epictetus, who preached against money, in return for being paid. Like the catalogue in 'The Library of Babel', we might say that the Zahir does not so much impose order as 'repeat disorder'. The underlying principle that the Zahir represents is not to be seen directly; but the very disorder and heterogeneity of the world itself, all that is not the Zahir, is now only possible because of the Zahir.

### 'THE ALEPH'

'The Aleph' is widely regarded by critics as the greatest of all Borges' stories. Originally appearing in *Sur* in September 1945, it was subsequently included as the final piece in the collection *El Aleph*, which appeared in 1949. Despite this, Borges has wondered in the notes he published for the English-language translation of 'The Aleph' in 1970 whether the story was too 'ambitious' (*A*, 170). It is a judgement that critics have by and large rejected, praising the story instead for its richly detailed setting, its deftly sketched characters, the balance it achieves between earthy humour and sublime vision and the wide variety of writerly tones it seamlessly incorporates. The story, like 'The Zahir', is in many ways a lament for a lost or impossible love. Biographers differ as to whether its subject is Norah Lange, Borges' great passion of the 1920s, or Estela Canto, whom Borges was still seeing at the time but of whose affection he could never be sure. Regardless of the true subject of the story, Borges gives this biographical fact brilliant resonance by naming his heroine after the character Beatrice in Dante's *Divine Comedy*, an allusion that both gives the story a universal grandeur and opens up a satirical, mock-heroic distance on to its subject matter. Borges also offers us in the figure of the buffoonish poet Carlos Argentino Daneri at once a witty portrait of the pretension and provincialism of Argentine literature at the time and an unsparing self-assessment of his creative achievement to that point. The story shares many features in common with 'The Zahir'; but 'The Aleph' is invariably judged to be the more successful of the two stories, and critics have even opposed them in terms of their respective attitudes towards the possibility of an underlying principle to the world.[9] ('The Zahir' is understood to be realist and 'The Aleph' nominalist.) We might not disagree with this literary judgement, but we would argue that the two stories are essentially the same in their logical structure and what they have to tell us about the relationship between realism and nominalism and the one and the many.

'The Aleph' begins, like 'The Zahir', with the narrator, also called Borges, recalling the death of a woman, Beatriz Viterbo, with whom he had once been in love. Remembering that it was her birthday, he decides as a way of keeping her memory alive to visit her parents' house and pay his respects. He takes a melancholy pleasure in reacquainting himself, as he waits in the parlour, with the many photographs of Beatriz, taken from different angles and recording the various episodes in her life. Thereafter Borges – who is depicted in the story as a lonely and at best semi-successful writer – takes the opportunity to visit each anniversary of Beatriz's birthday, with the convention slowly developing that he would be invited to stay for dinner. Over the years, he gradually makes the acquaintance of Beatriz's first cousin, Carlos Argentino Daneri, who also lives at the house. Daneri, a handsome, dandyish man – who works, like Borges did, in a small library on the southern outskirts of Buenos Aires – takes the opportunity to confide in him his literary ambitions, and even reads out to him a section of a long-winded, lugubrious epic poem entitled *The Earth*, which proposes no less than to set the entire surface of the globe to verse. What Daneri reads to Borges is at once pretentious, Victorian in style and seemingly never-ending, and is inevitably accompanied by Daneri's own self-justifying and self-congratulatory commentary. Nevertheless, as Borges admits, by 1941 Daneri had

> already dispatched several hectares of the state of Queensland, more than a kilometre of the course of the Ob, a gasworks north of Veracruz, the leading commercial establishments in the parish of Concepción, Mariana Cambaceres de Alvear's villa on Calle Once de Setiembre in Belgrano, and a Turkish bath not far from the famed Brighton Aquarium. (*CF*, 277)

Matters come to a head when Daneri, after having previously asked Borges' help in securing an 'attention-getting recommendation' (*CF*, 279) for the forthcoming publication of the first part of his epic, rings him up in a panic to tell him that the landlords of his cousin's house are about to demolish it, along with its 'Aleph', the object he had been using to help him write his poem. When Borges asks him what an 'Aleph' is, Daneri replies simply: 'One of the points in space that contains all points' (*CF*, 280). Borges' curiosity piqued – and half wanting to prove Daneri mad or an imposter – he agrees to come over and see this 'Aleph' Daneri is talking about. Arriving at the house, in a parodic inversion of the topography of Dante's *Divine Comedy*, in which enlightenment is to be gained by ascending, Borges following Daneri's instructions descends into the cellar beneath the house. Daneri's instructions to Borges are very precise. It seems that the Aleph can be seen only from one particular point of view. It is necessary to lie on the floor of the cellar with one's head supported by a burlap bag and focus on the nineteenth step up. Humorously – it serves to lighten the mood of what follows – Borges, as he lies there in the dark trying to focus on a point he cannot yet see, suddenly realizes that he is at the mercy of a madman. He is locked in a dark cellar, with someone whose poetic ambitions he has snubbed and who will soon be exposed as a fraud when his 'Aleph' fails to appear. Then, as Borges' eyes gradually adjust to the dark, he sees it.

What then follows is a long, rapturous description of what Borges sees in the Aleph. It is one flowing, unbroken sentence that draws on, as Borges has acknowledged, the long-breathed parataxis of Walt Whitman, one of Borges' favourite poets in his youth. The passage has also, as critics have pointed out, something of the visionary or apocalyptic qualities of the Biblical *Book of Revelation*. It is one of the most cited and celebrated passages in all of Borges' writing, although it is oddly untypical of his style:

Under the step, toward the right, I saw a small iridescent sphere of almost unbearable brightness. At first I thought it was spinning; then I realized that the movement was an illusion produced by the dizzying spectacles inside it. The Aleph was probably two or three centimetres in diameter, but universal space was contained inside it, with no diminution in size. Each thing (the glass surface of a mirror, let us say) was infinite things, because I could clearly see it from every point in the cosmos. I saw the populous sea, saw dawn and dusk, saw the multitudes of the Americas, saw a silvery spider-web at the centre of a black pyramid, saw a broken labyrinth (it was London), saw endless eyes, all very close, studying themselves in me as though in a mirror, saw all the mirrors on the planet (none of them reflecting me) . . . saw in a study in Alkmaar a globe of the terraqueous world placed between two mirrors that multiplied it endlessly . . . saw a Persian astrolabe, saw in a desk drawer (and the handwriting made me tremble) obscene, incredible, detailed letters that Beatriz had sent Carlos Argentino . . . saw the circulation of my dark blood, saw the coils and springs of love and the alterations of death, saw the Aleph from everywhere at once, saw the earth in the Aleph, and the Aleph once more in the earth and the earth in the Aleph. (*CF*, 283–284)

After this ecstatic and overwhelming vision Borges wreaks his revenge on Daneri by not letting on that he has seen anything. He then concludes his tale – and this should remind us of 'The Zahir' – by saying that after a few sleepless nights, he was eventually able to forget the Aleph. In a postscript, he adds that the house in which the Aleph was located was eventually demolished. He wonders how Daneri came up with the name for the Aleph, which in the Kabbalah is the first letter of the Hebrew alphabet and in mathematics is used to represent the number of elements in an infinite set, and speculates that he may have read it in one of the innumerable texts that the Aleph itself revealed to him. He then goes on to make the following surprising allegation. He proposes that the Aleph under Daneri's stairs was a *false* Aleph. His evidence – and we might recall that series of objects throughout history that have been a Zahir in 'The Zahir' – is a manuscript by the British consul to Brazil in the mid-1800s, Sir Richard Burton, in which he records the variety of objects that throughout history have been thought to reflect or contain the world. Burton begins his account by recording several literary examples, such as the mirror attributed to Alexander the Great, a goblet of the Kai Khosru, a mirror in *1001 Nights*, a reflective spear attributed to Jupiter in *Satyricon* and the mirror of the magician Merlin in Spencer's *Faerie Queen*. But Burton lists these examples only to conclude that the true Aleph is to be found inside one of the stone columns of a mosque in Cairo. As he writes: 'No one, of course, can see it. But those who put their ear to the surface of it claim to hear, within a short time, the bustling rumour of it' (*CF*, 285). Borges then concludes his tale with the melancholy thought that he can no longer recall whether he did in fact see the Aleph, just as he can no longer remember the features of his beloved Beatriz's face.

So what exactly, we might ask at the end of all of this, *is* the Aleph? We might say that, before all else, the Aleph is a way of seeing the world, is nothing else but the necessity of a certain perspective on to the earth. This is brought out by the way that, in the story, Daneri is so particular about where Borges has to lie in order to see the Aleph; that there seems to be just one place from which to view it correctly. Looking at the Aleph is like looking through a peephole or looking at something from a particular point of view. Indeed, lying in the dark and looking at its screen might remind us of the cinema (and we know that Borges was a keen cinema-goer and reviewed films throughout the 1930s). Or the Aleph might remind us of a kaleidoscope (and we know that Borges at the time he was writing the story was very much taken with a kaleidoscope, which he nicknamed his Aleph). And yet, insofar as we are able to see the Aleph, insofar as we are able to look through the Aleph, the Aleph itself must also be *inside* the world. As Daneri explains, it is 'one of the points *in space* that contains all points'. In other words, exactly insofar as we come to see the Aleph, that from which all else is seen, there needs to be another Aleph outside of that, which looks upon both the Aleph and the world it sees, and so on. This is why Borges, writing with his customary rigour even at the height of that long rhapsodic passage, concludes with: 'I saw the earth in the Aleph, and the Aleph once more in the earth and the earth in the Aleph', in a reversal or circularity that could go on forever.[10]

What is opened up here – as we have seen throughout Borges – is a form of logical regress or recursion. As soon as we see the Aleph, or see the world through the Aleph, there is implied another point of view that would allow us to see *that*. In a sense, like the catalogue in 'The Library of Babel', every Aleph is divided into the Aleph that sees the world and the Aleph that is seen in the world. Hence Borges' suspicion that the Aleph Borges sees in Daneri's cellar is a *false* Aleph, insofar as it would have to be seen from another 'true' one. What is suggested here, of course, is an endless series of such Alephs, each making visible the one before. It is for this reason that the final, apparently 'real' Aleph on Burton's list must not only must remain invisible but also is constitutively split, existing only as a representation or rumour of *itself*. And, most brilliantly when we actually go back to the list of objects seen in Daneri's cellar, each of these also has the quality of being at once what allows us to see and what is seen, what stands outside of the world and what exists only within it: eyes, mirror, globe, astrolabe. Indeed, more than this, each already reflects upon itself and reflects upon itself through *an other*: eyes studying themselves in Borges; mirrors reflecting themselves across a globe between them; the book Daneri has read speaking about Alephs . . . Each object in the Aleph is already an Aleph, as any Aleph exists only within another Aleph. And it is *this*, finally, that allows us to think how the Aleph is 'infinite', as it is described as being several times in the story. The 'Aleph' is neither simply an object in this world (for this object would not exist without some outside point of view upon it) nor an Aleph (for the Aleph as this point of view can be seen only in the form of an object), but the very *relationship between* them. We might attempt to represent this diagrammatically:

$$\text{'Aleph'} \left\{ \quad \frac{\text{Aleph}}{\text{earth}} \right.$$

As we can see, at each turn in the relationship between the Aleph and the earth a new Aleph is required in order to see the previous relationship. As each successive Aleph is produced, it is in a sense the 'same' Aleph seen differently. It is this that explains the subtle theme of perspectivism that runs throughout the story. At the beginning of 'The Aleph', when Borges is standing in the hallway of Beatriz's old house, Beatriz in those old photos of her is seen in 'profile', in 'full-front' and in 'three-quarters' view (*CF*, 274–275). Similarly, when Borges is attempting to evoke the experience of the Aleph, he speaks of how it is like an angel 'facing east and west, north and south at once' (*CF*, 282). Later, when he is describing the Aleph itself, he speaks of the way that 'each thing was different things because I could see it clearly from every point in the cosmos' – and this includes the Aleph itself, which he sees from 'everywhere at once'. It is a perspectivism that is not so much of different views on to some object outside of them, as in Leibniz, as of different views on to an object that does not exist outside of these views, or that arises as a kind of self-division within them, the fact that they can never entirely be equal to themselves. It is a splitting within the Aleph, the fact that there always needs to be another in order to see the equivalence between it and the world, that produces the endless variety of things in the world. In a paradoxical way, what comes together in the Aleph is precisely the highest, that for which everything stands in, and the lowest, the endless list of objects in the universe. And it is this, to conclude, that explains Borges' disregard of Daneri and his poetry, beyond any jealousy he might feel for Daneri's closeness to Beatriz. In some ways, of course, their poetic ambitions are similar: Daneri's quest to versify the entire planet in a poem called *The Earth* is not altogether different from the ecstatic list Borges produces trying to evoke the experience of the Aleph. But what Borges realizes, which Daneri does not, is that the world and thus the poem recording it can never be literally infinite. Rather, the world and the Aleph are infinite only because of something outside of them. It is neither the Aleph nor the world that is infinite but only the *relationship between* them. And it is this relationship that Borges' description of the Aleph, unlike Daneri's, seeks to capture. What he describes is not so much the Aleph or the world the Aleph allows us to see as us seeing the world through the Aleph. What 'The Aleph' wants to make us perceive is perception itself, just as 'The Zahir' tried to represent representation. The Aleph is infinite because it represents the world, but the world is infinite only because it is represented by an Aleph.

## 'FUNES, HIS MEMORY'

The last of the so-called 'fictions of infinity' we consider here is 'Funes, His Memory', originally published in *La Nación* in May 1942. The story was written during an extremely productive eight-month period from mid-1942 when Borges completed most of the stories that formed the *Artificios* that augmented the original edition of *El jardín de senderos que se bifurcan* to become *Ficciones*. In fact, as with so many of Borges' stories, 'Funes' was an elaboration of a speculation originally put forward in a piece of non-fiction. In this case, it was the essay 'A Fragment on Joyce' (*TL*, 220–221), originally published in *Sur* in February 1941, which wondered at the prodigious powers of retention required for a reader to hold all the references of James Joyce's *Ulysses* in mind at once while they read the book. On a more biographical level, Borges described the story, which concerns a man who perceives the things of this world with an overwhelming, crystalline clarity and is subsequently unable to forget them, as an allegory for the 'severe insomnia' he suffered throughout his life. It is a clarity that Borges was all the more aware of, insofar as it was around this time that his eyesight began seriously to deteriorate and he became conscious of the need to store up memories against the day when he could no longer see. Undoubtedly, however, the issue that has dominated the critical reception of the story is the long-running philosophical dispute between realism and nominalism. It is an opposition explicitly raised by the narrator towards the end of the story (*CF*, 136–137); and, in trying to decide where Borges' own sympathies lie, critics have pointed out that in the second edition of *A History of Eternity* Borges admits that, although previously he did not see the need for classificatory universals in order to think, he now does (*OC* I, 351). But, as we have already argued, rather than taking sides in these kinds of intellectual disputes, Borges' preferred method – it is this that we would say defines 'fiction' for him – is to render the opposition inoperative, reveal that neither side of the opposition is possible without the other. It is this that we see in 'Funes', even against perhaps the narrator's own position.[11]

'Funes' takes the form – as it will turn out, ironically – of a testimony or reminiscence, intended to be published in a small volume dedicated to the subject of the story. As part of his contribution, our narrator recalls meeting the young Uruguayan *gaucho* Ireneo Funes three times. The first time was in February or March 1984, when the narrator was riding a horse with his cousin in Fray Bentos during his summer holidays and they were forced to find shelter during a storm. When his cousin sees a young boy walking nearby, he asks him what the time is. Without looking at a watch, the boy is able to reply without hesitation: 'Four minutes till eight' (*CF*, 132). It is Funes, who was already famous in his village for his ability to tell the time without referring to a clock. The next occasion the narrator sees Funes, it is some three years later, when he returns to Fray Bentos for his summer holidays. He learns that Funes had been thrown off a horse and is now crippled. He is confined to a bed, from which he never moves. Funes hears of the narrator's presence in town and asks to borrow from him some books in Latin and a Latin dictionary, even though he has never studied the language before. The narrator consents, even though he is a little annoyed at Funes' apparent belief that he could pick up Latin so easily. The narrator is then suddenly called back home a few days later when he learns his father is unwell, and goes to collect his books from Funes. He is astounded when he arrives at Funes' house to hear him flawlessly reciting a passage from Pliny's *Natural History* that deals with memory. The last words of the chapter from which he recites are 'ut nihil non iisdem verbis redderetur auditum' (*CF*, 134), which can be translated as 'nothing is heard that is not repeated in the same words'.

Our narrator then pauses before coming to the heart of his story and apologizes for his own faulty memory. He is not directly able to remember the words that Funes spoke to him all those years ago – curiously, given the copy of Pliny he was carrying with him then – but is able only to 'summarise faithfully' (*CF*, 134) what he said. He also asks the reader to imagine the 'broken and staccato' (*CF*, 134) rhythms and pauses in the conversation, which he can reproduce only as though it occurred without a break. Funes begins by recalling for the narrator all of the cases of prodigious memory that Pliny enumerates in his book: a king who could name all of the soldiers in his army; a ruler who could speak all twenty-two of the languages of the territories he held. But Funes himself wonders what is so remarkable about these cases. Before his accident, he was, as he says, like everyone else, 'blind, deaf, befuddled and virtually devoid of memory' (*CF*, 134). Now, he claims, his memory is perfect. He forgets nothing. As our narrator puts it:

> He knew the forms of the clouds in the southern sky on the morning of April 30, 1882, and he could compare them in his memory with the veins in the marbled binding of a book he had seen only once, or with the feathers of spray lifted by an oar on the Río Negro on the eve of the Battle of Quebracho. (*CF*, 135)

As ordinary humans can grasp the form of a circle, a triangle or a rhombus when drawn on the blackboard, so Funes could intuit the form of the stormy mane of a colt, a small herd of cattle on a mountainside, a flickering fire and its ashes and the many faces of a dead man at a wake. Indeed, such is the sharpness and specificity of Funes' memory that he rejects even those previous schema of nominalism proposed by such thinkers as the English empiricist John Locke, in which every stone, bird or branch of a tree would have its own name. These, extraordinarily enough, Funes discounts as being too general, too ambiguous. Rather, as our narrator explains: 'Funes remembered not only every leaf of every tree in every patch of forest, but every time he had perceived or imagined that leaf' (*CF*, 136). Indeed, Funes is unable to grasp not only that the general category 'dog' should apply to dogs of different breeds and sizes, but even that the 'dog' seen at 3.14 in the afternoon in profile should be given the same name as the same dog seen at 3.15 from front on. In a similar way, his own face and hands surprised him every time he saw them. Such was Funes' visual acuity that he was able to track the slow advances of decay, corruption and weariness that humans suffer. He was able to perceive all of the minute changes in our bodies that occur as we move inexorably towards death.

As some attempt to come to terms with this overwhelming capacity to remember, Funes tried several times to classify his memories and perceptions. On two or three occasions, he sought to reconstruct an entire day. He had forgotten nothing, but the reconstruction itself had taken an entire day. He devised a new numbering system, supposedly meant to save time, in which a compound number was replaced by a single figure or word. For example, instead of 7013, he would say 'Máximo Pérez'; or, instead of 500, he would say 9. He then attempted to reduce his past to some 70,000 memories, which he would then classify by numbers. However, as our narrator adds: 'Two considerations dissuaded him: the realisation that the task was interminable, and the realisation that it was pointless' (*CF*, 136). Surrounded by a constant barrage of memories that were as strong as any original impression, Funes finds it impossible to enter into that state of distraction or inattention required for sleep. Even in the darkness of his room, he is able to visualize 'every crack in the wall, every molding of the precise houses that surrounded him' (*CF*, 137). In order to get to sleep, Funes would turn towards a newly built part of the city that was unfamiliar to him or imagine himself at the bottom of a river. Indeed, the conversation that our narrator recollects for us occurs over one long night when Funes was unable to get to sleep. The narrator remembers the dawn sun rising and catching sight of Funes, who although only nineteen looked ancient. Some two years after his meeting with the narrator, Funes dies of pulmonary congestion – a peculiarly appropriate disease, critics have noted, for a man so overloaded with accumulated memories.

Funes' problem certainly seems to be a surfeit of memory that cannot be classified or otherwise got rid of. It would be as though Funes perceived and memorized everything, down to the finest particulars, so that no generic category or distinction remained. And yet what we see is that what makes this infinity, this overwhelming difference, possible is a certain limit or generalization, even if we can put it this way a certain blindness or forgetfulness. Let us begin, for example, with Funes' own complaint: that the word 'dog' is inadequate not only for all of the different types of dog, but even for the same dog seen at 3.14 in profile and at 3.15 from front on. The implication is that the world is made up of an endless variety of such canine-related phenomena with nothing, not even the concept 'dog', that they are all variations of. And yet, of course, we would not even be able to remark upon the fact that these phenomena *were* different unless they could be compared to each other or otherwise had something in common. The same thing can be seen with the idea that, beyond even those empiricists who argued that every stone, bird or branch be given a different name, Funes believed that 'every leaf of every tree in every patch of forest', 'every time he had perceived or imagined' it, be given a different name. Here again, the very singularity of experience being spoken would require a certain limit, something that is *not* subject to the same process of endless difference that everything else is. For, we might ask, what exactly is it that constitutes the unity of that 'leaf', that 'tree', that 'patch of forest' and, indeed, of the different 'times' in which it is seen or perceived or imagined? There is a boundary that must be drawn around each of these categories, implying some kind of unity or integrity, that would precisely allow comparisons to be drawn and distinctions to be remarked. And the same objection would apply even to the notion that Funes can actually perceive decay, corruption and the slow progression towards death. Here too, for all of the implication that everything is running down, that nothing remains the same, something must remain unchanged, some unity must persist across which alteration can be seen to have occurred: the same face, the same hands, the same body.

As Borges' more insightful commentators observe, Funes' observations do not in fact constitute an unbroken sequence of indiscernible differences but more a number of 'static slices, a series rather than a continuum'.[12] What they mean by this is that we never actually have that minute incremental advance spoken of by the text, but only a passage between two discrete points *across* which change must be assumed to have occurred. We can divide up the movement of things in space or the passing of moments in time as closely as possible, but we would always miss the actual moment of transformation. The further division of space and time is always possible, just as any stated ideal or category can always be broken down; but any further division could occur only between limits, just as we could break down one concept only by replacing it with another. That is to say, this difference can take place only within an overarching category of the *same*. And Borges makes this 'limit' very clear in his text. As the critic Sylvia Molloy was the first to observe, the narrator's first presentation of Funes during his stay at Fray Bentos is 'cut off' from the rest of the story, forming a kind of static visual image that is separate from the rest of the narrative.[13] Indeed, as the narrator admits, he repeats his conversation with Funes without those 'broken and staccato periods' that testified to the impact Funes was having on him as he listened. Ironically, however, it is this very abstraction that creates such a remarkable portrait of Funes, just like those other *exemplary* figures in Pliny's catalogue. It is only within this overall context, which precisely allows us to generalize and even to compare similar examples, that this story of Funes' infinite memory is able to be presented in a way that has any significance to us.

To go back to the argument of this chapter, however, we would say that, just as it is a certain sameness that allows Funes to remark upon difference, so this sameness could only ever be presented in an always different form. The truly subversive aspect of Funes and his refusal of those general categories of not only the circle, triangle and rhombus, but also the stone, bird and branch is that it reveals to us that we too never experience these general categories as such, but only ever encounter an overwhelming heterogeneity of different phenomena with seemingly nothing in common between them. In a sense, like Funes, the clouds in the sky remind us of the veins in the marbling of a book, which remind us in turn of the splash created by an oar on the river; but we cannot say what they *all* remind us of, and any attempt to say what they have in common – to produce a memory of memory, as it were – produces only another phenomenal example that for the reasons we have seen above is *different* from those others. This, of course, is the paradox of memory as exposed by Funes. We have a memory because something reminds us of something else. Memory is never singular but always a comparison between two. But every attempt to say what these two have in common, to say what the memory is a memory of, produces only another memory, something that because it has to be remembered in the world is different. This is the futility of Funes' attempts to classify his memories, and why he could never finish doing so: because, insofar as the classification of his memories would have to be in turn remembered, he would need another memory of *that*, and so on. The ultimate key to memory, what all memories are a memory of, is always missing; every memory is merely a memory of another memory.[14] In that way we have seen before, then, memory is neither of some individual thing (because we do not have a memory at all unless it reminds us of something else) nor of what two things have in common (because any attempt to say what this is would produce only another memory), but the very *relationship between* them. And it is precisely because this 'memory of memory' is always missing, because we can never say what all our memories are memories of, because there is something we *cannot* remember, that memory is infinite, that our world is made up of an endless set of memories. We might attempt to represent this diagrammatically:

## STUDY QUESTION 1

A number of critics have spoken of the way that 'Aleph', after which that 'small iridescent sphere of almost unbearable brightness' (*CF*, 283) is named, is not merely the first letter in the Hebrew alphabet, but also a kind of 'space' or 'breath' preceding all letters or language as such. (See on this Lisa Block de Behar, 'Rereading Borges' "The Aleph": On the Name of a Place, a Word and a Letter', *The New Continental Review* 4(1), 2004, pp. 169–187.) Why is this particularly appropriate given the logic of the story?

## STUDY QUESTION 2

Borges outlines in 'Avatars of the Tortoise' Aristotle's famous argument of the 'third man', which is the idea that in positing any category that two or more things have in common we would always need *another* category, which both that category and those things have in common. At the end of his demonstration, Borges suggests that in fact we do not need two or more things to produce this situation: 'it is enough to have one individual and the general type in order to determine the *third man* denounced by Aristotle' (*L*, 239). How might we think this logic of the 'third man' at stake in the Borges' stories we have looked at here? More specifically, with regard to 'Kafka and His Precursors', 'The Library of Babel', 'The Zahir' and 'The Aleph', how is it a matter not of two or more things but of 'one individual and the generic type' that produces this infinite regress of the 'third man'?

## CHAPTER 5

# READING THE SHORT STORIES: FICTIONS

Borges spoke often of the distinctive power he attributed to fiction. As a reader, he wrote of the transformative effect certain books had on his own life. As a critic, he championed a select, slightly out-of-date group of authors he particularly admired (Chesterton, Stevenson, Kipling, Wells). And as a writer, he admitted that he could not finish, let alone attempt to emulate, the work of many of the great early modernists (James Joyce, Ezra Pound). All of this gives us some clue as to the kind of fiction that Borges sought to produce himself: the tale, the short story, what the French call the *récit* and the Spanish call the *cuento*. It is not a record of psychological development, in which the subject's character is revealed through a series of dramatic incidents. It is not an account that plays on narrative distance, the subtle shifting relationship between the writer and their characters. To this extent, Borges' fictions would be the antithesis of the 'realism' of Émile Zola and Gustave Flaubert. But they also could not be understood as one of the experiments in authorial voice inaugurated by such writers as Henry James and E.M. Forster. On the contrary, as opposed to the slow, controlled development and sense of inevitability in those authors, as though the end of the story is reached in fulfilment of some objective social law or moral or literary truth, Borges constantly emphasizes the element of surprise, of unexplained narrative reversal, in his fiction. At once everything in his stories is directed towards the end; but this end when it arrives opens up an entirely different reading of everything that came before, which remained hidden until that moment. The model here is not the 'realism' or 'naturalism' of the nineteenth-century French *roman* or the internal psychological drama of the twentieth-century English novel, but the conceptual wit and brevity of the eighteenth-century French *conte* and the self-enclosed artificiality of the twentieth-century American detective story. As Borges writes in his essay 'Narrative Art and Magic', contrasting these two different approaches to fiction:

> I have described two causal procedures: the natural or incessant result of endless, uncontrollable causes and effects; and magic, in which every lucid and determined detail is a prophecy. In the novel, I think the only possible integrity lies in the latter. Let the former be left to psychological simulations. (*TL*, 82)

It is for this reason that Borges' own fictions became the founding case for the critical category of 'metafiction' and were seen to pioneer the literary genre of 'magical realism'. Metafiction in its most general terms could be defined as the exploration of 'the relationship between the world *of* the fiction and the world *outside* the fiction'.[1] Magical realism in its turn could be said to be characterized by 'the matter-of-fact, realist tone of its narrative when presenting magical happenings'.[2] Certainly, throughout his writings Borges was conscious of the constructedness of the worlds he was creating and interested in exploring the conventions that defined fictional as opposed to other kinds of writing. As we have seen already in 'The Garden of Forking Paths', 'The Immortal', 'Pierre Menard' and 'The Library of Babel', Borges in his stories frequently incorporates actually existing books, documentary facts and himself and his friends as characters in the attempt to confuse fictional and non-fictional writing. Similarly, in such stories as 'The Zahir' and 'The Aleph', we have seen an element of the fantastic enter and corrupt quotidian reality without it being explained in terms of dream or hallucination or any other supernatural rationalization. It becomes unclear in Borges' stories – and, as we have seen, this is one of their deepest subjects – what is real and what is unreal. As David William Foster says of this metafictional aspect of Borges' work: '[It] is metaphorical of the process of fiction, both on the external level of man's creation of systems as well as on the internal level of man's creation of literary artifices'.[3] And as Suzanne Jill Levine says of Borges' role as the progenitor of Latin American magic realism: 'Borges drew the line between the old and the new . . . by inventing a new – soon to be labelled 'postmodern' – concept of fiction'.[4]

These are undoubtedly important insights into Borges' work, but we can be more specific still in elaborating what Borges means by fiction and the particular power he attributes to it. There is more at stake here than the simple collapse of the distinction between reality and fiction or the intrusion of the fantastic into the everyday. In fact, if we look carefully at the Borges stories we have examined so far, we notice a very specific narrative economy. What we read is at once the effect and delay of the phenomenon of which it speaks. We might give just one example of this. 'The Zahir' begins with the narrator describing an obsession he knows will eventually consume him so that he will be unable to think of anything else. How the story will end is evident in almost the opening words of the story. And yet the narrative – which in a way *is* the very obsession the narrator speaks of – is also the endless deferral of this inevitability. As long as the narrator can continue to speak of the Zahir, we know that he has not completely fallen under its spell. And we see the same thing in each of the Borges narratives we have looked at: in 'Forking Paths', everything exists as only one of the infinitely many possibilities produced by the labyrinth, except for the narrative that speaks of this; in 'The Library of Babel', everything is subject to the rules of the Library, except for the story in which we read about it; in 'The Aleph', the entire world is contained within the Aleph, except for the point of view that allows us to see this. Because of this 'contradiction', the narratives of Borges' stories have a very specific temporality: neither the linear unwinding of events from the beginning to the end nor even the retrospective re-reading of events from the end back to the beginning, but the infinite deferral of an event that has already occurred. Of course, we return here to the narrative logic of something like *1001 Nights*, an absolute touchstone for Borges; and beyond that to his particular understanding of Zeno's paradox, in which similarly the end can be endlessly deferred, but only because we have already reached it. It is something Lisa Block de Behar speaks of as the temporality of 'retrospective anticipation' that marks Borges' fictions, and Sylvia Molloy as the 'interpolation' that makes them up, in which something 'opens the text up in the middle' between two points.[5] In this sense, the event Borges' fictions narrate never actually occurs, but the narration itself is proof that it already has. And it is this, finally, that Borges means

by fiction: not the collapse of reality into fiction but the aware-
ness that reality is possible only insofar as it stands in for a
fiction. It would be a fiction that precedes and will eventually
take over reality, but that can be narrated and made conscious
only insofar as reality persists. We take up in more detail what
Borges means by 'fiction' through a close reading of two texts
here: 'The Lottery in Babylon' and 'Tlön, Uqbar, Orbis Tertius'.

## 'THE LOTTERY IN BABYLON'

'The Lottery in Babylon' was originally published in *Sur* in
January 1941, and then included in *The Garden of Forking Paths*,
which came out the same year. It is, along with 'The Circular
Ruins' and 'The Library of Babel', one of the three major texts
that Borges wrote during this time. It is a period characterized
by Borges' continued depression at his dead-end job as a shelver
at the library, the fact that he was still living with his mother
and, according to one biographer, the existential fear that he
did not exist. And, indeed, all three of these stories are characterized by a certain 'abstraction', an almost comic vision of the
futility of humans trying to make sense of the world. Borges, in
fact, explicitly admits the influence of Kafka on 'The Lottery of
Babylon', and the story has the feel of such parables as 'The
Great Wall of China' and 'Josephine the Singer, or The Mouse
Folk', in which Kafka evokes on a grand, cosmic scale faraway
and ancient civilizations, whose absurdities cast light on our
own. However, as Borges acknowledges in the 'Foreword' to the
original edition of *Forking Paths*, the story is also 'not wholly
innocent of symbolism' (*CF*, 67) of a much more contemporary
kind. It is well known that Borges followed the course of the
European war being waged at the time very closely. He wrote
a series of stories, such as 'Deutsches Requiem', 'The Secret
Miracle' and, as we will see, 'Tlön, Uqbar, Orbis Tertius', where
it is used either as a backdrop or explicit reference; and he
authored a number of essays on various aspects of the war,
which he published in *Sur* and the weekly *El Hogar*. In many
ways, 'The Lottery in Babylon' can be described as an allegory,
'after Kafka, of totalitarianism'.[6] It was a totalitarianism that
those living in Argentina at the time had to face not only from a
possible Axis victory, but also in a home-grown form, with the
sidelining of President Roberto Ortiz in 1940 and his replacement

by Ramón Castillo, who was entirely under the control of the right-wing and Nazi-endorsing army. Indeed, extending the political reading of the story, it has even been noted that the acronym in Spanish of the mysterious Company that runs the lottery in the story is CIA. Some critics, nonetheless, have not been convinced by Borges' turn to political allegory, and complex debates have taken place over the exact nature of the politics that Borges' fictions (as opposed to his real-life statements) represent. For example, the fact that the lower classes in 'The Lottery in Babylon' willingly choose to give up their freedom by participating in the Lottery has been seen by some as not unconnected with Borges' own later controversial contention that Argentina was not ready for democracy, and that for the time being it was best governed by a benevolent dictator.[7] However, complicating this elitist reading of the story, it would also have to be admitted that it is the *lower classes* in this particular case that rise up and force the upper classes to obey their will.

'The Lottery in Babylon' is the story of how a lottery in the distant country of Babylon, while starting off like any other lottery we are familiar with, gradually expands to take over all aspects of reality. It is told by a narrator who relates his story in the 'little time' (*CF*, 104) remaining before the ship for which he is waiting takes him back to his homeland. He begins by speaking of the way his father told him that centuries ago – although whether this is true the narrator admits he cannot be sure – the lottery was a simple affair conducted by barbers, in which in exchange for copper coins participants entered a draw in which the winners won coins made of silver. However, as the narrator suggests, this early version of the lottery was a failure because it did not appeal to all of the faculties, but only to people's sense of hope. In order to widen the attraction of the lottery, a number of unlucky outcomes were thus distributed amongst the lucky ones. Now people entered the lottery because they did not want to be considered cowards, although there were needless to say those who entered and lost but were reluctant to pay their fine. The Company therefore decided that, instead of handing out fines, they would send unlucky ticketholders straight to jail. It was subsequently determined, both for the sake of the symmetry and because money did not necessarily guarantee happiness, that the winners would be rewarded not with prize money but with other, more direct forms of compensation. As a result – in a kind of parody of political enfranchisement – the lower classes of Babylon, who were unable to afford to buy a ticket in the Lottery, demanded the right of inclusion. At one point, a slave stole a ticket, which brought upon its bearer the loss of their tongue. As luck would have it, this was also the punishment for stealing a lottery ticket. Faced with this coincidence between the lottery and the real, the masses won their argument over the opposition of the well-to-do, and the right to participate in the drawings of the Lottery of Babylon became universal.

The power of the Company running the lottery in these new circumstances became vastly more expanded. Because every citizen in Babylon was automatically entered in the lottery, the Company was forced to take over all public power. Drawings were held every sixty days, and entirely determined a citizen's fate until the next drawing. And the possible outcomes of each such drawing became exponentially more complicated. For example, a lucky draw might bring about somebody's happiness or it might bring about somebody else's unhappiness. It might bring about election to high office or a woman arriving at one's room. It might bring about one's enemy's dishonour, mutilation or death. But with the rising of the complexity and sometimes the seeming remoteness of the outcomes of the drawings, people were increasingly tempted to believe that what had happened was simply the result of chance. In order to counter this, the Company sent agents out into the field in order to make people believe that the Company was behind everything. And the people in turn were encouraged to believe that they could actually communicate with the Company. However, this inducing of people to believe that the Company was responsible for every aspect of the world, and could even control chance, made the Company realize that it should actually involve itself in every aspect of their lives and not just in some of them. Thus in time *everything* concerning Babylonian citizens' lives became subject to the drawings of the lottery. Not only were rewards and penalties decided upon, but also who should execute them, how they should be distributed, whether they should at the last moment be reversed, and so on. As the narrator puts it: 'The number of drawings is infinite. No decision is final; all branch into others' (*CF*, 105). At this point, when the number of drawings becomes in practice 'infinite', the lottery becomes identical to life itself. The supposed chance and indetermination of the world seem to coincide entirely with the necessity and determination of the lottery.

Indeed, as the narrator goes on to remark, beyond the personal there are soon even *impersonal* drawings, which involve not merely humans but also things in the world. For example, a drawing might decree that a sapphire is to be thrown into the river, a bird is to be released from captivity or a grain of sand is to be added every hundred years to a beach. Now, every single aspect of Babylonian life is caught up in operations of the lottery. When we buy wine, we can never be sure whether inside the bottle is a good luck charm or a snake. Scribes who write out legal documents invariably introduce errors. There are even, our narrator admits, some errors in what he has said to us; he has undoubtedly misrepresented, whether inadvertently or not, some aspect of the Company's operations. Babylonian historians, for their part, have found ways of taking this into account; but not without introducing themselves new errors, or involving themselves in new practices of deceit or cover-up. Indeed, there is nothing so prone to uncertainty as the history of the Company itself. For example, it cannot be decided whether an archaeological document that relates to its past is genuine or the result of a drawing from past centuries or even more recently. No book on the Company is published without some discrepancy between copies. Researchers take a secret oath to omit, interpolate within or otherwise alter what they discover. 'Indirect falsehood', presumably also regarding matters concerning the Company, is practised. Now, it simply cannot be determined what is and what is not the result of the Company. Might not a drunk shouting or a man murdering his wife be the following of some obscure command or directive of the Company? In fact, several competing hypotheses concerning the Company continue to circulate, between which the narrator cannot decide. It is possible, some suggest, that the Company ceased to exist hundreds of years ago and its rules and rituals are merely hereditary. It is possible, suggest others, that the Company is omnipotent and will last until the end of time. It is possible, suggest still others, that the Company is omnipotent, but has decided to exert power only over small, inconsequential things: the crying of a bird, the shades of rust and dust, the dreams that come to us at dawn. It is possible, suggest a minority, that the Company never did exist. And it is even possible, finally, that we cannot decide whether the Company ever existed or not, because Babylon is 'nothing but an infinite game of chance' (*CF*, 106).

'The Lottery in Babylon' can obviously be seen as a forerunner to such contemporary television shows as *Big Brother* and *Loft Story* and such films as *The Matrix* and *The Truman Story*, in which every aspect of reality is artificially constructed and manipulated, without the protagonists entirely knowing what is going on. It is not altogether surprising that science-fiction enthusiasts see some affinity with Borges because 'Lottery in Babylon' – as well as, we will see, 'Tlön, Uqbar, Orbis Tertius' – reads like one of those classical paranoid fantasy scenarios, in which behind the apparently benign surface of everyday life a gigantic and ultimately unprovable conspiracy is taking place. Or, of course, in another of Borges' long-running interests – we might recall here the dedication with which Teodelina followed the dictates of fashion in 'The Zahir' – the situation of 'The Lottery in Babylon' might remind us of certain 'primitive' societies, in which every aspect of personal behaviour is strictly controlled and prescribed. And all of this is taken to an extreme extent as the lottery increasingly takes over all areas of Babylonian society and resembles the world itself. *Everything* eventually becomes subject to the lottery and its drawing and redrawing of lots, with the ultimate result that not only are the number of drawings in effect 'infinite' but no particular drawing is final, with it always being possible that another will come along after it to correct or withdraw it. This has the effect, as the narrator notes, that our very ability to know about the lottery is an outcome of the lottery. The Company sends agents out into the field to influence people's opinions; historians, while correcting some errors, inevitably introduce others; it cannot be decided whether the archaeological evidence speaking of the origins of the lottery is a product of the lottery. Everything we say or think, including about the lottery, might be the result of one of the drawings of the lottery, might be merely the following of the instructions on one of its tickets.

The analogy here – quite obviously so with Borges saying that 'no decision is final; all branch into others' – is with 'The Garden of Forking Paths'. As with Ts'ui's labyrinth there, what the idea of a lottery does is make everything an effect of the lottery, including whether we know of it or not. As one of the heretical cults of Babylon suggests at the end of the story, to know and not to know of the lottery are equally the effect of 'chance'. They are both the possible outcome of a drawing of the lottery, and thus are subject to the kinds of errors introduced by the lottery, are able to be reversed or withdrawn by another such drawing at any moment. Even the narrative we read – the account given by the narrator as he waits for a ship to take him back to Babylon – itself possibly misrepresents aspects of the lottery, consistent with the practices of Babylon, as the narrator admits. Indeed, the narrator himself could even be one of those agents sent out into the field, hoping to influence people's opinions about the lottery. And yet, just as in 'The Garden of Forking Paths', all of this would be possible only because we *do* know about the lottery. There would be one thing, for all of the lottery's infinitely branching paths and way that everything is subject to cancelling out and correction by subsequent possible drawings, that could not be different, and that is the narrator speaking to us about the lottery. There would be one thing that is not liable to the possibility of either deliberate or inadvertent error, direct or indirect falsehood, and that is that the narrator is telling us the truth about the lottery. For all of the idea that the drawings of the lottery are 'infinite' or at least 'infinitely subdivisible' (*CF*, 105), so that we could never get to the end of them, all of this infinity can be seen only looking back, arises only as a retrospective possibility of the discovery or narration of the lottery.

And yet, of course, as in 'The Garden of Forking Paths', no sooner is the hypothesis of the lottery posed than this outside or end can be seen only as an effect of the lottery. Once more, the narrator speaking truthfully from somewhere outside of it can seem like one of those infinitely many alternative destinies produced by the lottery. *Every* document concerning the lottery carries the errors and falsehoods introduced by the lottery, including the narrative we have before us. In this sense, despite Borges' brilliant unravelling of all of the logical consequences of the lottery, in the end it is not a matter of the suspenseful extrapolation of an initial premise, of reality gradually being taken over as successive aspects of human existence fall under the operations of the Company. Rather, as soon as the very notion of the lottery is announced, it is all over. It is no longer possible to ascertain any outside reality or any moment that comes before the lottery. We see this exactly at those moments in the story in which the Company dramatically 'increases' (*CF*, 102) its powers. When the Company, instead of sending to jail those who refuse to pay the fines on their tickets, introduces tickets that just directly send people to jail, what is being made clear is that those fine defaulters were in effect *already* playing the game. Similarly, when a slave has his tongue cut out for stealing a ticket, which is incidentally the punishment corresponding with holding that ticket, again what is being made clear is that the slave was *already* playing the game. And yet, if these instances point towards the fact that there is no limit to the lottery – that legal sanctions are only alternatives within the lottery, that everybody is already playing in the lottery – in another way they do in fact point to a limit to it. For they are telling us that we can never know the lottery as such but only through the *exceptions* to it. We become most aware of the lottery, and indeed of the fact that it has always been, precisely when its rules are being broken. Every attempt to speak of the lottery only produces another error, introduces another misconception. But this itself can be said only from the point of view of a 'lottery' whose rules we *do* know and whose truth *can* be stated. We might attempt to represent this diagrammatically:

$$\text{'Lottery'} \left\{ \frac{\text{Lottery}}{\text{Babylon}} \right.$$

To say all this more slowly: the lottery as it expands gets closer and closer to life. Everything, even the smallest details of Babylonian reality, is seen to be subject to the draw of the lottery: the cry of a bird, the shades of dust and rust, the dreams that come to us at dawn. But the real point here is that we would not even notice these things until the lottery. One of the meanings of the narrator speaking of the taking-over of reality by the lottery is that things suddenly appear significant because they are now subject to the lottery. The notion of an infinite or infinitely divisible lottery serves to divide the continuum of experience up, to mark one thing off from another, insofar as it might belong to a different draw from it. It is to re-mark the things of this world as though from somewhere else. Each thing shines forth in its individuality because it could now be other-wise, because it could not be at all if the draw had turned out differently. It is not that the lottery actually changes anything about the world, for all of the alternatives supposedly opened up by it, because things could only have turned out the way they did; but the lottery is the very *possibility* of things not being as they are, of a kind of void or absence running beneath things for which they stand in, that must be understood as making the world visible to us. And it is this void or absence that precedes all attempts to speak of it, and makes of any such attempt an exception, an error, a falsehood. It is not the lottery but only takes its place, arises as an effect of it. This again would be the idea that the world has become the lottery, so that we can no longer tell what is real and what is not, or even whether the lottery exists or not. And yet, precisely insofar as we are able to think that the world has become a lottery, this lottery *can* be known inside the world, as exception, error, falsehood. If we cannot tell whether the world is real or whether the lottery exists, we can at least know *this*. Paradoxically, insofar as we can still say that the world has become a *lottery*, the true principle of the 'lottery' has not yet taken over the world. In this sense, the lottery, if it is what precedes all narration and makes of it an exception, is also a name for narrative itself and is itself this exception.

### 'TLÖN, UQBAR, ORBIS TERTIUS'

The last story of Borges we consider here is 'Tlön, Uqbar, Orbis Tertius', which was originally published in *Sur* in May 1940, and subsequently went on to become the first story in *The Garden of Forking Paths* when it appeared in 1941. It is undoubtedly one of the stories for which Borges is best known. It has been widely reprinted in literary and science-fiction anthologies, and it is the story that Mick Jagger reads a section aloud from in the bath when he plays a gangster in the film *Performance*. It is one of the stories, along with 'The Garden of Forking Paths', 'Pierre Menard' and 'The Aleph', that has inspired the most admiration and commentary from Borges' critics. For example, the critic

Martin Stabb in his survey of Borges' stories describes 'Tlön 'as a 'tour de force of literary gamesmanship';[8] and biographer James Woodall speaks of Borges in 'Tlön' 'deploying astonishing narrative forces . . . an elaborate intellectual conceit, existential fear and numerous, teasing autobiographical reference points'.[9] As Woodall implies here, 'Tlön' is frequently seen as the most autobiographical or at least 'Borgesian' of Borges' stories, the one in which he comes closest to outlining his genuine literary and philosophical beliefs. The idealism of the imaginary land of Tlön, as outlined in the *Encyclopaedia* devoted to it in the story, is said to represent Borges' own idealism. And the notorious remark in the 'Postscript' to the story expressing a certain distance towards both 'Nazism' and 'dialectical materialism' is also said to represent Borges' own quietist liberalism, a lack of political commitment for which he has often been criticized. However, in both of these regards, the text is not quite so straightforward as it might appear. If Borges *does* put forward his own beliefs in 'Tlön', it is only – and this is exactly one of the powers he attributes to fiction – to question them, suspend them, show that they are possible only because of what is opposed to them. Equally, if Borges is understood to reject both Marxism and dialectical materialism because of their ideological extremism, the logic of fiction Borges advocates in their place is revealed to be far more extreme in its ambition to take over the world.

As we say, 'Tlön', perhaps for the very reason that it is seen to be close to Borges' own personal beliefs, has inspired more academic commentary than virtually any other Borges story. 'Tlön' is inevitably read in terms of the philosophical doctrine of idealism, which is specifically featured at several points in the story. Indeed, the eighteenth-century English philosopher George Berkeley is even named as one of the members of the conspiracy that gives birth to Tlön. Commentators also detect traces of a pantheism – the idea that a single God or spirit infuses every part of the world – that was associated with the nineteenth-century German philosopher Arthur Schopenhauer, who is one of the thinkers that Borges has said was most important to him. Beyond this, the subject of a secret society dedicated to inventing or discovering a higher or hidden truth behind appearances has allowed some to interpret Borges' story as an expression of his 'esotericism', his belief in a mystical or occult explanation of the world that can be known only to a group of initiates. The critic Didier Jaén, in a book devoted to the topic, puts this most acutely when he wonders whether the story is 'a parodic history of the transformation of the world under the influence of [the seventeenth-century secret society] the Rosicrucians'.[10] Along similar lines, critics have seen the imaginary world of Tlön, which Borges elaborates in great detail in the story, as indicating a certain 'utopian' impulse in Borges' work. This has been viewed positively by such critics as James Irby as exercising a 'process of 'negative thinking' that keeps us 'aware of the conjectural character of all knowledge and all representation".[11] However, it has also been viewed negatively by such post-colonial critics as Beatriz Sarlo as a 'conservative' attempt to produce a pure and unmixed world of the imagination in the face of the heterogeneous racial and social mix of the region in reality.[12] 'Tlön' has even been described by critics as a 'parody' of the regional novel, in effect, of magic realism, before the genre as such was invented.[13] Equally contradictorily, the novel has been read both as a not-so-subtle metaphor for the potential takeover of the world by the Axis forces, which at the time were making great advances across Europe, and a highly deliberate and self-conscious reflection on the operation of fiction itself. At the same time, that is, Borges could say a few months after the publication of the story and perhaps by way of explanation, 'each morning, reality resembled more and more a nightmare',[14] and the story can be understood as a 'partial allegory of the emergence of Borges' fiction over the years'.[15] Nevertheless, with regard to the latter interpretation, it would be too much to argue, as some critics have, that it is in 'Tlön' that Borges 'exhibits most forcefully the contention that reality cannot be distinguished from fiction'.[16] In fact, as we will see, the true argument of the story is that fiction can never entirely become identical with reality; that if reality is possible only because of a certain fiction, this fiction for its part can never definitively be realized.

The story starts off, in a much-cited beginning, with the narrator, whom we take to be Borges, having dinner with his old friend Bioy Casares (Adolfo Bioy Casares, as we know, was a real person, a lifelong friend and literary collaborator of Borges). During their conversation, Bioy repeats a saying he remembers from one of the 'heresiarchs of Uqbar' to the effect that 'mirrors and copulation are abominable, for they multiply the number of mankind' (*CF*, 68). When challenged by the narrator as to the source of this epigram, Bioy says that it comes from the entry on Uqbar in his 1917 edition of *The Anglo-American Cyclopaedia*, which is a 'literal reprint' of the earlier 1902 edition of the better-known *Encyclopaedia Britannica*. A copy of the *Cyclopaedia* is found in the house in which the narrator is staying, but a search of it fails to turn up the reference, or indeed any mention of Uqbar itself. The next day Bioy rings Borges up to tell him he has found the reference to Uqbar in his copy of the *Cyclopaedia*, although he had misremembered the original quotation, which is slightly longer. The narrator then says that he would like to see Bioy's copy, which is discovered to be exactly the same as the narrator's, except for the extra pages at the end of one volume that are devoted to Uqbar. Together the narrator and Bioys read the entry. It strikes them as very much like a typical encyclopaedia entry, covering the various aspects of the region's geography, history and literature, although it is marked by a certain vagueness regarding specifics. The only memorable aspect of the entry regards Uqbar's literature, which it notes is one of fantasy, insofar as it never refers to reality but rather to the two imaginary realms of Mle'khnas and Tlön. The bibliography for the entry lists four references, which cannot be found, although one does figure in another catalogue, and the narrator later finds the author of another referred to by Thomas De Quincey as a theologian who described an imaginary community named 'Rosy Cross', which others then founded in imitation of it (*CF*, 70). Further enquiries by the narrator fail to turn up any similarly altered copies of *The Anglo-American Cyclopaedia* or any further mention of Uqbar.

There the matter rests, until two years later when the narrator returns to the hotel at Androgué at which his family used to stay and finds in the bar a book originally sent to Herbert Ashe, an old friend of his father who had recently passed away. When he opens the book, he is astonished to find that it is a volume of 1001 pages written in English, entitled *A First Encyclopaedia of Tlön. Vol. XI: Hlaer to Jangr*. In this volume – seemingly just one of many – there is described in vast and exhaustive detail the life, beliefs and culture of one of those two imaginary realms, Tlön, that was mentioned in the original entry on Uqbar in Bioy's copy of *The Anglo-American Cyclopaedia*. It is the exposition of the content of this volume that the narrator undertakes in the second half of the story (and it is the narrator's summary of the contents of this volume that critics claim to be an expression of Borges' personal beliefs). The narrator begins by noting that the various nations that make up the planet of Tlön are, 'congenitally, idealistic' (*CF*, 72). Their languages, religions and metaphysics all presuppose idealism. Thus for the citizens of Tlön the world is made up not of objects in space that persist over time, but of a series of successive and temporally independent acts, with no necessary relationship to each other. There are thus no nouns in the various languages of Tlön. In the southern hemisphere, there are verbs modified by adverbs, so that instead of 'The moon rose above the river' we have 'Upward, behind the onstreaming it mooned' (*CF*, 73). In the northern hemisphere, by contrast, we have a series of adjectives strung together to form momentary unions made up of two or more terms, such as the colour of the sun and the distant cry of a bird or the feeling of sun and water against our chest while swimming, together with the pink we see when our eyelids are closed and the sense of being caught up by a river and by sleep. These unions can be put together with others to form longer combinations. Indeed, there are in the northern hemisphere of Tlön whole poems made up of a single, unbroken word.

There are therefore in Tlön, insofar as there is no subsisting empirical reality, no sciences but only psychology. The causal explanation of an event or the linking of one action to another is seen to be merely a retrospective reconstruction by the subject and not to have anything to do with the actual event being explained. For example, the successive perception of a cloud of smoke, the countryside on fire and a half-extinguished cigarette is understood not to imply any necessary causal connection, but to be an instance merely of the association of ideas. Similarly, every attempt to give any of these mental states a name is considered to introduce a 'distortion', a 'slant' or 'bias' (*CF*, 74) into them. The paradoxical result of this absence of objective truth is not so much the absence of metaphysical systems as their overwhelming proliferation. But, again, the aim of these various systems of thought is not to discover the truth, but rather to amaze, astound or produce something beautiful. As the narrator puts it: 'In their [Tlönian philosophers'] view, metaphysics is a branch of the literature of fantasy. They know that a system is naught but the subordination of all the aspects of the universe to one of those aspects – *any* one of them' (*CF*, 74) – although, as he immediately notes, the phrase 'all the aspects' here should be avoided, to the extent it implies a continuity between the past and the present that would otherwise not be allowed. Perhaps of all the Tlönian thought-experiments none more amazed or astounded than the doctrine of materialism. In one particularly provocative example – intended as a contradictory demonstration of something self-evidently impossible – it is proposed that on Tuesday X loses nine copper coins along a deserted road. On Thursday Y finds four coins on the road, on Friday Z finds three on the road, and on Friday morning X finds two on the veranda of his house. This sequence of events caused a scandal in idealist Tlön because it implied that the same coins somehow persisted throughout the period when they were lost and were therefore no longer perceived. Various solutions to the enigma were proposed, including the argument that the very words 'lost' and 'found' as used in the problem were inadequate, insofar they assumed they were the same coins, the very issue that was in contention. Fortunately, a solution more fitting to Tlön's pantheism was eventually found: that the universe is but a single subject and the various objects in it are its masks or organs. Thus Y and Z find the coins because they remember that X has previously lost them, and X for his part finds two coins on his veranda because he remembers that the other coins had already been found.

Along the same lines, the narrator speaks of the way that this doctrine of a single, all-encompassing subject plays itself out in literature (again, this aspect of the story is invariably read as a statement of Borges' own beliefs, with commentators drawing a connection particularly to 'Pierre Menard' and 'The Garden of Forking Paths'). In Tlönian culture, it is decided that all books are the work of a single author, so that critics will often take two dissimilar books – say, the *Tao Te Ching* and *1001 Nights* – and attribute them to the same author. In the same way, literature is understood to have but a single plot, although it is given with every possible permutation. For similar reasons, every book also comes with its own refutation, and any book that does not contain its own counter-argument is considered incomplete. Finally, the narrator outlines, in one of the most discussed aspects of the story, the Tlönian notion of *hrönir*: objects that appear in reality as a result of people's expectations and preconceptions. In the ancient regions of Tlön, two people might be looking for the same pencil. The first person finds it, but does not tell the other. The other finds a second pencil, no less real than the first, but more in keeping with his expectations, and differing from the first only in being slightly longer than it. Now these *hrönir* are sought to be deliberately produced in Tlön. In one early experiment, prisoners were shown a photograph of what they were going to find on an archaeological dig, with the promise that whoever found what was in the photograph would be set free. Of course, all that was found after a week's excavation was a rusty wheel dated from some time *after* the experiment. But a later experiment involving the students of a high school *was* successful, with them finding – or producing – a gold mask, an ancient sword, two or three clay pots and the mutilated torso of a king. This synthetic production of *hrönir* is of great benefit to Tlönian archaeology, insofar as it enables researchers not only to investigate the past but also to modify it. However, as opposed to the *hrönir*, which are produced by expectation, there is also the phenomenon in Tlön that objects tend to vanish when they are no longer seen or thought about. An example of this – Borges here is paraphrasing Kafka's famous parable 'Before the Law', which he had translated some two years before – is a doorway that was lost when the beggar who frequented it died, and sometimes an entire amphitheatre has been kept present through the perception or recollection of a few birds or horses.

Thus the narrator's tale ends with this long disquisition on Tlönian life, as outlined in the eleventh volume of *A First Encyclopaedia of Tlön*. The narrator had previously canvassed the debate that occurred between scholars as to whether this eleventh volume was in fact the only one. Certainly, up until the point at which the story ends, it is the only one discovered. It is even suggested by some scholars that they should themselves complete the remaining volumes of the *Encyclopaedia*, based on the hints provided by the volume they know of. But in a postscript said to be added in 1947 – impossibly, seven years *after* the original story was published in *Sur* – the narrator goes on to reveal that in March 1941 a letter was found in a book once belonging to Ashe, in which the truth about Tlön was revealed. In the early seventeenth century, a secret society (one of whose members was George Berkeley) was founded with the aim of inventing a country, along with all of its customs, philosophical systems and religious beliefs. After several years of work, its members realized that one generation would not be enough to accomplish the task. In 1924, in Memphis, Tennessee, one of them met the reclusive millionaire Ezra Buckley, who told him that, if the society decided to invent not a mere country but an entire planet, he would leave it his fortune. In 1914, the final volume of the *First Encyclopaedia of Tlön* was complete. But this undertaking, astonishing as it was, was itself understood to be the basis for another, even more comprehensive work, this time to be written not in English but in one of the languages of Tlön, to be entitled *Orbis Tertius* (it is 'Orbis Tertius' that was stamped on the frontispiece of the volume that was discovered at the hotel, as though it were already a product of this as yet non-existent stage). After the discovery of this letter sent to Ashe, events proceeded quickly. In 1942, a Princess who was unpacking her tea service that had been sent from France discovered a strange compass stamped with letters from one of Tlön's alphabets. Some months later, a young *gaucho* who died on the Brazil-Uruguay border was discovered with a strange cone-shaped object, made out of a metal no one could identify, which was in the image of one of the Tlönian deities. Then in 1944 all forty volumes of *The First Encyclopaedia of Tlön* were discovered in a Memphis Library. Some of the more outlandish features of the original volume eleven had been modified – particularly the idea of deliberately bringing about *hrönir* – and the *Encyclopaedia* made a huge impact. Translations, summaries and commentaries soon spread throughout the world in great numbers. This, along with the continued appearance of Tlönian objects, meant that human reality soon 'caved in' (*CF*, 81). Now, as the narrator writes, the original Tlönian language is taught in schools and Tlönian history has replaced the earthly one. The human sciences have been transformed by their contact with Tlön, and even mathematics and biology await their transformation. In one hundred years from now, when *The Second Encyclopaedia of Tlön* appears in its own language, the narrator speculates, all the other languages of the world will disappear. The world will become Tlön. The narrator himself, in the haunting last lines of the story, indicates that he has returned to the hotel in which he originally found the eleventh volume of the *First Encyclopaedia* and works on a translation, which he intends never to publish, of Sir Thomas Browne's *Urne Buriall*.

As we say, one of the first questions to put to 'Tlön' is, to what extent does the world proposed in the *First Encyclopaedia of Tlön* represent Borges' own beliefs? It is undoubtedly true that Borges often spoke of idealism, and throughout his writings praised the great philosophers of the idealist tradition, a number of whom are specifically mentioned or alluded to in 'Tlön': Plato, Berkeley, Kant, Schopenhauer, Spinoza. Indeed, the influence of a number of minor figures in the tradition can also be detected there: Hans Vaihinger, Fritz Mauthner, Macedonio Fernández. But, as the story itself suggests, no book in Tlön – including presumably the *Encyclopaedia* – is complete without its opposite or counter-book. And, as we have ourselves argued, this 'dialectic' has been Borges' own preferred method throughout his career, if we can indeed attribute anything of 'Tlön' to Borges' own beliefs. Accordingly, if the world of Tlön is one of 'congenital idealism', Borges also shows that this idealism would not be possible without its corresponding materialism. We see this, to begin with, in Tlönian poetry, in which in both southern and northern hemispheres, despite the notion that there are only successive states of being, objects are seen as being simultaneous or otherwise in relation with each other. In the southern hemisphere, the adverbial qualification of verbs creates a situation in which two things are seen as connected with each other, as in 'Upward, behind the onstreaming it mooned'; in the northern hemisphere, the putting together of adjectives produces *metaphor*, a state of likeness between two, as in the comparison between the colour of the rising sun and the cry of a bird or the feeling of the sun and water on a swimmer's chest, the pink produced when we close our eyes and the sense of being swept along by a river and by sleep. We see the same thing with the famous coin experiment, in which in order to sustain the argument that the same coin does not remain between being lost and found, we need to suppose either a single substance that the coins are modifications of or a pantheistic spirit that the various finders of the coins are the earthly avatars of. It is this necessity for an underlying, but never accessible, reality that is also implied by the Tlönian insistence that the naming of such things as mental states inevitably introduces a 'distortion', 'slant' or 'bias'. For, although this reality is never available insofar as every naming of it would be to distort it, we nevertheless could not even say that it *was* a distortion unless this reality existed somewhere. We see the same thing, finally, in the argument that the aim of every intellectual system in Tlön is the subordination of 'all the aspects' of the universe to any *one* of those aspects. Not only, as the narrator remarks, does this assume the very thing that this metaphysics seeks to disprove – namely, a subsisting reality outside of these metaphysical hypotheses – but, as we have seen throughout Borges, it opens up the thought that this hypothesis is itself 'one of these aspects', and that an infinite regress would be implied insofar as another hypothesis would be required to subordinate *this* hypothesis, and so on.

We can see this 'contradiction' – a certain materiality allowing idealism – also in the *transmission* of Tlön, the series of events that leads to this secret society's imaginings taking over the world. It is said in the *First Encyclopaedia*, consistent with classic Berkeleyian idealism, that things exist only insofar as they are perceived. This is what the verbs and adjectives of the various Tlönian languages attempt to capture; it is why causal explanation is understood as an example of the association of ideas; it is why there is no linear, successive time in Tlön; and it is why Tlönian objects lose detail and even cease to exist when there is no one to perceive or remember them. And yet, as certain critics have pointed out, the conspiracy that ends up producing Tlön proceeds underground unnoticed from its first meetings in the early seventeenth century until the meeting with Ezra Buckley in 1824, and then again from this meeting until the narrator first notices that aberrant encyclopaedia entry. Similarly, against a metaphysics that would argue that the world is not a joining of objects in space but a series of independent and successive acts with no connection between them, it is notable that the very generation of Tlön relies on the 'conjunction' of a mirror and an encyclopaedia; and that, later in the story, the second intrusion of Tlönian reality in the form of a cone-shaped object that slips from a gaucho's belt arises from a 'coincidence' (*CF*, 80).

More profoundly, the very possibility of *hrönir* themselves – objects that arise out of expectations – also requires a certain persistence in time, a holding in mind of past events in order to produce something in the future. Indeed, even the ability, as the narrator says, of *hrönir* to 'modify the past' (*CF*, 77) through the production of archaeological artefacts seems to violate Tlön's injunction against temporal succession. More than this, in the idea that *hrönir* can either prospectively appear in the future or retrospectively modify the past there is implied not only the idea of a future and past but a future and past in themselves that are not merely the effect of *hrönir*. In order to assert the idealist notion that the future and past are only effects of the *hrönir*, there must necessarily remain a future and past to which we can compare them. Finally, at the conclusion of the narrator's story, when he tells us that the world has become Tlön, he says that 'the rest lies in every reader's memory (if not his hope and fear)' (*CF*, 80), again necessarily assuming both the reality and temporality that Tlön would do away with.

It is at this point that we come to the complex question of the narration of 'Tlön', and how this relates to the general problematic of fiction in Borges' work. Like 'The Lottery in Babylon', 'Tlön' is often seen as a masterfully narrated story of the slow taking-over of reality by the alternative principle of Tlön. Critics speak of 'the feeling of a slowly growing nightmare, of accumulating unrealities that become all-embracing',[17] as at first an encyclopaedia entry, then a volume of an encyclopaedia, then several objects, then an entire encyclopaedia appear from this other place, until at last reality gives way and the world becomes Tlön. But, of course, in another way, like 'The Lottery in Babylon', once we reach the end of the story, we realize that the true point being made is that the world is *already* like Tlön; that for the story to be told at all the conspiracy has been in place from the outset, pulling the strings and ensuring that Tlön will be realized. As the narrator himself suggests, it is perfectly possible that the discovery of the full Tlönian *Encyclopaedia* in Memphis in 1944 was not accidental but brought about by the mysterious directors of 'Orbis Tertius'; and the fact that the frontispiece of the single volume originally discovered was stamped with the words 'Orbis Tertius' indicates that this third and final stage of the conspiracy was already present on earth.

But, indeed, as more perspicacious critics have pointed out, even from the beginning of the story the Tlönian principle of *hrönir* is at play, insofar as it could be understood that when Bioy finds that quote in the *Anglo-American Cyclopaedia* (revealingly, a little 'longer' than the original) it is exactly in expectation of finding evidence for his witticism after first coming up with it at the dinner table. And, of course – it is this the narrator aims at when he writes that scholars at one point considered finishing the Tlönian *Encyclopaedia* based on the single volume discovered so far – our world *is* like Tlön, to the extent that the human knowledge that makes it up proceeds like a giant conspiracy fabricating a world from scratch. The earthly arts and sciences proceed also through the imagining of a world, the finding of *hrönir*-like objects that match their hopes and expectations. And, moreover, in any attempt to think this Tlön-like process in which objects come to match a prior expectation, there is always an expectation before *that*. We can never get to the bottom of the Tlönian conspiracy because it precedes and makes possible all attempts to investigate how it came about. And yet, as we have seen in 'The Lottery in Babylon' and other Borges stories, we nevertheless *can* think the Tlönian conspiracy. We *do* become aware of it, which is indeed the only reason why we can also think how we cannot think how it came about. We might attempt to represent this diagrammatically:

$$\text{'Tlön'} \left\{ \frac{\text{Tlön}}{\text{reality}} \right.$$

The enigma of Tlön might be put this way: Tlön is what the world stands in for. The story is about a certain *hronir* or conspiracy that precedes the world and brings it about. In this sense, we might say that the story is an allegory of representation and the idealist notion that the world is its own representation. Fundamentally, the world is unreal, takes the place of something we cannot name – not even as 'representation' – because every attempt to name it is preceded by it, arises as an effect of it. And yet this very insight of Borges at his most esoteric, mystical, religious and idealist would not be possible without a certain thinking of *this*. Tlön exists only within the world, and when we say that Tlön has taken over the world this can be said only from a position outside of it, from some other reality that is *not* Tlön. This is the material converse to Borges' idealism: that this single unchanging substance for which everything stands in can be seen only through the infinitely heterogeneous things of this world. We have then the same infinite regress that we saw in the idea that Tlönian metaphysics is the subordination of 'all the aspects' of reality to 'one of those aspects', in that this 'one aspect', insofar as it is part of reality, must be subordinated to yet another, and so on. It is to suggest at once that there is one aspect to which the rest of reality is subordinate and that the process of finding it will go on forever, insofar as there must always be another from which it is seen or narrated.[18] The miracle of fiction, then, is its ability, at least for a moment, to single out one of these aspects. Even though what will be revealed is that this single thing stands in only for another and that it can be seen only from reality, for a moment it can operate as the hidden explanation of the world, that through which everything else must be understood. Fiction is neither the simple statement of facts from which an explanation can be generated nor even the re-reading of those facts in the light of a new explanation, but the sudden invention of a *name*, after which both the facts and their explanation exist as though for the first time.[19] Labyrinth, immortality, Kafka, copy, Library, Zahir, Aleph, Lottery, Tlön: all of these are miraculous *doublings* of the world. After them, we can think only in terms of them. The world can be conceived only in light of them. And yet they themselves in their commonality only stand in for something else, some 'logic' that we have tried to trace throughout here and that makes them possible. This 'logic' is both what precedes all representation and exists only in representation. It is at once utterly transcendental and entirely worldly. It at the same time comes before all narrative and is strictly equivalent to the exact words of Borges' stories. This most abstract and unnarratable of logics can be seen only in Borges' choice of words, selection of theme and organization of material. It is what we meant by saying in our first chapter that we would attempt to read this logic through the details of Borges' stories and that these details would become visible only through the following of this logic. This logic certainly existed before Borges – it is the profound meaning of Borges' insistence on his 'unoriginality' – but it also reaches its purest and most concentrated expression in his work, which makes Borges perhaps the most singular and original author of the twentieth century, if not the entire history of literature.

## STUDY QUESTION 1

The critic Sylvia Molloy speaks about Borges' stories in terms of a certain logic of 'interpolation' (*Signs of Borges*, p. 100). What does Molloy mean by interpolation and how do we see it in Borges? Beyond those moments when the word is actually used in the stories we looked at (*CF*, 104, 115, 195), we might think also of that moment in 'The Aleph' when the narrator says as he is about to try to describe his experience of the Aleph: 'I now come to the ineffable centre of my tale' (*CF*, 282). How is the Aleph itself a kind of interpolation?

## STUDY QUESTION 2

Borges' work has often been described as quietist, traditional or even conservative in its emphasis on the long continuities of human civilization and the repetitions that seeming novelties reveal themselves as being. But taking up Borges' definition of the aesthetic fact as the 'imminence of a revelation as yet unproduced' (*TL*, 346), can we imagine Borges' work another way: as the attempt to set out the conditions for a certain literary and perhaps even political 'act'? In answering this question, students may wish to refer to Shlomy Mualem, 'The Imminence of Revelation: Aesthetics and Poetic Expression in Early Wittgenstein and Borges', *Variaciones Borges* 18 (2004), pp. 197–217.

# CHAPTER 6

# RECEPTION AND INFLUENCE

In his recently published collection of occasional writings, Turkish Nobel Prize-winning author Orhan Pamuk speaks of the way that Borges helped him at a certain critical point in his career. Pamuk is known for his series of densely plotted and richly textured novels, often set in the past, that take up amongst other things the interaction between East and West. Pamuk wanted as a young man to write in effect historical novels; but this seemed impossible at the time, both because of prevailing literary taste and because the social and political problems of contemporary Turkey seemed so much more pressing. After reading Borges, says Pamuk in an interview with *The Paris Review*, 'I realised I could go back to that [traditional Islamic] material with a Borgesian mindframe . . . so that I could easily appropriate its wealth of games, gimmicks and parables'.[1] The Portuguese Nobel Prize-winning author José Saramago has written a series of novels – like those of Defoe and Swift before him – that offer allegorical descriptions of events that affect whole societies. In *The Stone Raft* (1986), the entire Iberian peninsula becomes detached from mainland Europe; in *Blindness* (1995), all the inhabitants of an unnamed city are suddenly struck blind; and in the sequel *Seeing* (2004), the majority of people in an election spontaneously decide to cast blank ballots. In Saramago's 2005 *Death with Interruptions*, death suddenly stops taking place in a small unknown country and the people start living forever. It is a novel described by reviewers as having the 'strangely logical illogicality' of Borges and as having obviously been inspired by his 'The Immortal'.[2] The recently deceased Chilean novelist Robert Bolaño left behind at his death the massive incomplete novel *2666*. Coming in at some 898 pages in the English translation, this dense, metaphysically freighted behemoth created an immediate literary sensation, winning the 2008 American National Book Critics Circle Award and a large international readership.

It is a novel that one reviewer described as 'a tribute to, if not a rewriting of, Jorge Luis Borges' fictitious review cum short story "The Approach to Al-Mu'tasim"'.[3] And Bolaño, acknowledging this influence, once concluded a survey of Latin American literature he wrote simply by saying that 'one should read Borges more'.[4] In 2000 American wunderkind Mark Z. Danielewski published his first novel *House of Leaves*. At a time of rising experimentation in mainstream American fiction – David Foster Wallace's *Infinite Jest* (1996), Dave Eggers' *A Heartbreaking Work of Staggering Genius* (2000) and Michael Chabon's *The Amazing Adventures of Kavalier and Clay* (2000) – Danielewski's novel worked by the conceit that the events it spoke of could be arranged in different ways, and that even the pages of the book could be torn out and reshuffled. In footnote 167, one of the novel's several narrators, blind, elderly Zampanò (obviously a fictive stand-in for Borges himself) refers the reader to Borges' 'The Garden of Forking Paths'.

Today, as much as ever, Borges is with us. His books continue to sell in great quantities, literary critics continue to publish essays on various aspects of his work and his name continues to be cited publicly with regard to the most diverse and unrelated of matters. We might just offer here a brief overview. The American science-fiction writer Gene Wolfe has brought to life in his *Book of the New Sun* series two creatures from Borges' *The Book of Imaginary Beings*, the collection of mythological animals he put together with Adolfo Bioy Casares: the Baldanders, a monster that can adopt different forms; and an enigmatic 'fish' that can swim in mirrors. A recent anthology by Stefan Herbrechter and Ivan Callus, *Cy-Borges: Memories of the Posthuman in the Work of Jorge Luis Borges*, explores the connections between Borges' work and contemporary cyberculture and the new technologies of biogenetics. In the words of the editors: 'Not only could Borges be seen as one of the precursors of contemporary cyberculture, but also Borges' writing could be understood as a kind of "cyborg writing" as such'.[5] The 2006 film *Pan's Labyrinth* by Mexican director Guillermo del Toro is a chilling depiction of life in Franco's Spain, in which the young heroine periodically escapes from reality by entering an underground labyrinth, where she converses with all manner of mythological creatures. When questioned about the word 'labyrinth' in the title of his film, del Toro replied simply: 'I re-read Borges'.[6] The American artist Sherrie Levine, one of the pioneers of post-modernism in the visual arts, made her reputation through the direct copying or appropriation of other works of art. As part of the theoretical justification for the work – and in the style of the work itself – she often simply reproduces Borges' 'Pierre Menard, Author of the *Quixote*' as her artist statement. Indeed, in the spirit of Menard himself, her works have now been appropriated in turn by the artist Michael Mandiberg, in a project entitled *AfterSherrieLevine. com* (2001). Douglas Hofstadter, the best-selling author of *Gödel, Escher, Bach*, which examined the underlying connections between mathematics, art and music, published a few years later *The Mind's I: Fantasies and Reflections of Self and Soul* (1985), which raised issues about recursivity and self-reflection in the development of human consciousness. Although written in a popular style, the book could be seen as a precursor to the work of such cognitive scientists as Steven Pinker and Antonio Damascio, which similarly attempts to explain the emergence of human consciousness as the result of a paradoxical 'pulling oneself up by the bootstraps'. In making his argument, Hofstadter draws on two Borges texts in particular: 'The Circular Ruins' and 'Borges and I'. Finally, on one of the very technologies of the posthuman that Herbrechter and Callus discuss, YouTube, as well as the excellent Borges documentaries *The Mirror Man* and *Los secretas de un escritor*, there are also featured trailers for both real and imaginary films based on Borges' stories, people reading their favourite Borges stories to camera and even a woman performing a striptease using Borges' name as a keyword to attract viewers . . .

Of course, along with everything else published on Borges, there are also studies that take up the question of his reception and influence. A number of the biographies of Borges end with a chapter dealing with the fate of his work after his death or what James Woodall in his *A Man in the Mirror* calls Borges' 'afterlife'.[7] Several of the general surveys of Borges' work have chapters describing Borges' critical reception in some detail. Strong and accessible are the chapters 'The Critical Trajectory' in Martin Stabb's *Borges Revisited*, 'Critical Triumph and the Return to Tale-Telling' in Naomi Lindstrom's *Jorge Luis Borges: A Study of the Short Fiction* and the chapters 'Buenos Aires and

Beyond' and 'Literature and Politics North and South' in Gene H. Bell-Villada's *Borges and His Fiction*. There are as well a series of books that take up more specifically the question of Borges and his influence on literature. The first and most important of these is Edna Aizenberg's *Borges and His Successors*, published in 1990, which collects a number of essays exploring Borges' reception, in terms both of specific responses to or readings of his work (Italo Calvino, Michel Foucault) and the particular contexts in which his work has been taken up (Argentina, Germany, North America). Aizenberg's anthology was followed by the Norman Thomas di Giovanni-edited collection *The Borges Tradition* (1995) and the Spanish-language *La traición de Borges* (2005) by Marcello Simonetti. There are also a number of informative surveys that look at Borges' influence on succeeding generations of Latin American writers, such as Raymond Leslie Williams' *The Postmodern Novel in Latin America* (1995) and Juan E. De Castro's *The Spaces of Latin American Literature* (2008). There has as well been recently published *Reading Borges after Benjamin* (2007) by Kate Jenckes, which beyond looking at any actual influence passing between the two authors thinks rather how both were interested in a kind of 'messianic' history, in which traditions that had previously been written out or marginalized could be 'redeemed' through an act of critical reading.[8] This kind of possibility is also to be seen in a series of studies that consider Borges' relationship to the general problematic of translation. It is translation in these studies that is a metaphor both for what allows Borges access to the tradition he inherits and for the possibility of his own work living on in contexts that are not its own. The notion of translation as well allows critics to consider Borges' reshaping of tradition, the way he might be understood not simply to be reacting passively to the tradition he inherits but actively reshaping it in response to his own needs and situation. Several of these books are among the best things written on Borges. They are Daniel Cottom's *Ravishing Tradition: Cultural Forces and Literary History* (1996), with its extraordinary chapter 'Conspiring with Tradition: Jorge Luis Borges and the Question of the Miracle'; Efraín Kristal's *Invisible Work: Borges and Translation* (2002), which interprets a number of Borges stories as allegories of translation; and Sergio Waisman's *Borges and Translation: The Irreverence of the Periphery* (2005), which argues that it is the marginality of faraway Argentina that licensed Borges' creative misreading of the Western tradition.

The story of Borges' literary reception is well known, and told in one form or another in many of his biographies and the critical studies of his work. Borges mixed in ambitious literary circles from the very beginning. Upon his return from Europe in 1921, he brought with him not only the latest European styles but also a European ambition, a sense of the global – or at least European – stakes of artistic reputation. Back in Buenos Aires, Borges immediately launched into ceaseless literary activity, much of it keenly self-promotional, for all of the myth of him being shy and unworldly: founding small magazines, pasting up advertisements, inciting scandal and writing explanatory letters to newspapers. Borges was also prolific. During the 1920s, he published some three volumes of poetry and two volumes of critical essays. By the early 1930s, Borges was already a name to be reckoned with in advanced Argentine literary circles, and particularly for those with a European-trained sensibility. In 1933, the French writer and editor Pierre Drieu La Rochelle after meeting Borges in Buenos Aires was famously to say 'Borges vaut le voyage [Borges is worth the trip]'; the Polish exile and writer Witold Gombrowicz clearly recognized Borges as a rival and the literary magazine *Megáphone* as early as 1933 devoted an entire issue to Borges after his biography of *barrios* poet Evaristo Carriego. In 1931, Borges was selected to be part of Victoria Ocampo's *Sur* magazine, soon to be South America's most important literary journal (thanks in no small part to Borges himself). In December 1941, Borges went on to publish *The Garden of Forking Paths* with the *Sur* imprint. Its greatness was instantly recognized by those in his immediate literary circle. Bioy Casares, then a young man who had earlier met Borges through an admiration for his work, was to write at the time that the book opened up 'the literary possibilities of metaphysics'.[9] The Dominican critic Pedro Henriquez Ureña remarked in a much-quoted epithet that 'Borges would be original even when he proposes not to be'.[10] Both of these comments are extremely insightful for such a revolutionary work of prose, which effects an entire transformation in the field. But for this reason also Borges' stories did not win unanimous acceptance. In the 1942 Argentine National Awards for Literature, the book conspicuously failed to win a prize. Some of the judges were simply uncompre-hending. But others, even in their rejection, understood entirely the challenge it represented to the ruling literary establishment. In an anonymous report they released on the competition, they wrote: 'The jury felt it could not offer the Argentine people, at this time in the world, an exotic and decadent work which oscil-lates, in response to certain oblique tendencies in contemporary English literature, between the fantastic tale, boastful and recon-dite erudition and the detective story'.[11]

In fact, *The Garden of Forking Paths* had become more than just an extraordinary work of fiction. As the judges' report indi-cates, with its sinister anti-English xenophobia, this was a time of rising nationalism in Argentina. When the editors of *Sur* published their special issue '*Desagravio a Borges* [Amends to Borges]' and put on a celebratory dinner to compensate him for missing out on the Award, it was also a protest for a European cosmopolitanism against the fascism and anti-Semitism then sweeping the country. And if Borges was to serve as a figurehead for the cause, he was more than willing. During the war years, he was to write the powerful polemical essays 'A Pedagogy of Hatred', which is an analysis of the psychopathology of anti-Semitism; 'An Essay on Neutrality', which is a direct criticism of Argentina's professed stance of supporting neither side in the conflict; and the brilliant 'Defence of a Germanophile', which is an claim for the greatness of German culture against its Nazi perversion. Indeed, when Borges came to publish the augmented edition of *Forking Paths* as *Ficciones* in December 1944, and *El Aleph* in June 1949, the times were ready for him. The Argentine Society of Authors created a Grand Honorary Prize for *Ficciones*, and in 1950 Borges was himself elected to the Presidency of the Society. Also during the war years the French sociologist and publisher Roger Caillois had translated two of Borges' stories for the free France literary journal *Les Lettres françaises*, which in many ways laid the basis for Borges' later reputation in that country. In 1954, the first critical study of Borges' work appeared, Argentine Adolfo Prieto's *Borges y la nueva generación* (1954), which although largely uncomprehending does nevertheless acknowledge Borges' importance in Argentine letters. Three years later Ana María Barrenechea was to publish her *La expresión de la irrealidad en la obra de Jorge Luis Borges* (1957), which is a magnificent early expression of what we might call the New Criticism as applied to Borges. The 1950s were also a time of the first criticisms of Borges, from such writers and literary commentators as Ernesto Sábato and Jorge Abelardo Ramós. These denunciations were crude, couched in the familiar language of political 'commitment' and the necessity for nation-building; but later, more sophisticated criticisms would be made of Borges' politics, both in terms of his real-world actions and the strictly literary logic of his work. We might think here of José Eduardo González's *Borges and the Politics of Form* (1998) and Annick Louis' *Borges ante el fascismo* (2007). Perhaps more tellingly, there is the attitude that implicates Borges' eventual literary success in North America in the 1960s with an effectively apolitical conservatism:

> [The American literary elites] found in Borges' nightmares a sophisticated, inspired, vividly argued confirmation of their own stance [towards the Vietnam War]: that is, an urbane aloofness, a middle-way quietism, a studied, even-handed, occasionally snobbish indifference to right and left.[12]

This kind of criticism is revealing because it echoes that frequently made of literary deconstruction, which is also allegedly apolitical in its 'suspension' of binaries and emphasis on 'undecidability'. In fact, we would argue that many of the defences made of Derrida's work against such charges would apply also to Borges.

The year 1961 is said to be the real breakthrough year for Borges' international reputation. It is in that year that he shared the inaugural International Publishers' Prize, the Prix Formentor, which was the joint initiative of six major European publishing houses, with Samuel Beckett. As a result of this award, English translations were swiftly undertaken, with the best-of *Labyrinths* and *Ficciones* appearing in 1962, although Borges' work had already come out in French, German and Italian from as early as 1951. The first appearance of Borges' books in English created an immediate sensation. Major critics and literary figures devoted long, insightful and reverential reviews to Borges' work. The literary theorist Paul de Man in an essay for the *New York Review of Books* insightfully disengaged the themes of reversal and the coincidence of opposites in Borges' work. John Updike, writing as a novelist rather than a theorist, saw very clearly the fundamental realignment of the practice of fiction that Borges' work entailed. Indeed, Borges' work even influenced Updike himself, whose realist, character-driven epics of middle America would be almost its antithesis, when he started for a period in the mid-1960s to write short, absurdist miniatures, often accompanied by illustrations. And a whole slew of American writers (more so than the British at the time) explicitly drew on what they saw as the 'experimentation' of Borges: John Barth, Donald Barthelme, John Hawkes, William Gass and Gilbert Sorrentino. It is an influence that continues to this day, with such authors as Thomas Pynchon, William Gibson, Paul Auster, Don DeLillo, Sandra Císneros and Kathy Acker. In France, Borges has also had a major impact, both on the novel and on literary criticism and philosophy. The French New Novelist Alain Robbe-Grillet has not only produced a series of almost 'equivalents' to Borges' fictions in novel form, but in 1963 wrote the powerful literary polemic *For a New Novel*, which is one of the most complete followings through of the consequences of Borges' work for the practice of fiction. In terms of literary scholarship, Borges also as early as 1952 had essays written about him in the important journals *Critique* and *Les Temps modernes*; and in 1964 the prestigious monographic series *L'Herne* devoted an issue to Borges, which was effectively to canonize him in French intellectual circles. Later, the literary theorist Gérard Genette drew on Borges extensively to generate a new 'intertextual' theory of literature; and the philosophers Michel Foucault, Gilles Deleuze, Jacques Derrida and Jean Baudrillard have all either written on specific Borges texts or otherwise made his work not just illustrative of but inextricable from their theories. In Italy, the semiotician Umberto Eco saw in Borges' writings the basis for a radical theory of the 'open text', which would free the interpreter of all kinds of cultural objects from the controlling intentionality of their makers, the inherited distinctions of literary and cultural tastes and the institutional pressure to produce the 'correct' reading of texts.

Borges' reception in South America is in some ways more complex and ambiguous. Borges' stylistic austerity, his English understatement and his indebtedness to the French 'tale' made it difficult for a first generation of Spanish-speaking readers to follow him. Borges had also early on expressed his disdain for any kind of 'regionalism' in art (*TL*, 56–58). His opposition to or radical reinterpretation of Argentina's great poet Leopoldo Lugones and its great epic writer José Hernández was also a great wound to his country's narcissism. Later, his political mistakes or miscalculations – joining the Conservative Party, accepting an award from Pinochet – alienated him from all those sympathetic to the Left and the anti-imperialism movements of the 1960s and 1970s. Nevertheless, such Left-wing authors as the Chilean poet Pablo Neruda and the Colombian novelist Gabriel Garcia Márquez never thought to deny the greatness of Borges or the revolutionary effect he had on Latin American culture. All of the authors who constituted the 'boom' in Latin American literature of the 1960s – Julio Cortázar, Carlos Fuentes, Mario Vargas Llosa and Marquez himself – acknowledged the overwhelming debt they owed to Borges, both for their own work and for the very possibility of Latin American literature becoming visible. The hallucinatory precision and luxurious yet controlled verbal effects of 'magical realism' are not only clearly modelled on Borges' own prose, but were opened up as a literary possibility by such Borges essays as 'Narrative Art and Magic' (*TL*, 75–82) and 'The Postulation of Reality' (*TL*, 59–64) and their making available again such Spanish-language classics as Cervantes' *Don Quixote* and Enrique Larreta's *La Gloria de Don Ramiro* for a new generation of writers seeking to escape a European style. As well Borges' activities as a translator in making available such writers as Virginia Woolf and William Faulkner, whose work might be seen as having certain affinities with magical realism, additionally provided a subsequent generation of writers with the tools to renovate fiction. Today a wide 'diaspora' of Spanish-speaking novelists carry Borges' legacy with them, including the Argentine Luisa Valenzuela, the Puerto Rican Giannina Braschi, the Chilean Diamela Eltit and the Argentine Sergio Chejfec. Indeed, all kinds of Third World and post-colonial literatures draw on Borges and his practice and theorization of what might be called 'minor' literature: the Moroccan Tahar Ben Jelloun, the Arab-Israeli Anton Shammas, the British-Indian Salman Rushdie and the Australian Peter Carey. This is perhaps the true meaning of the 'Borges global' his biographers so often speak about.

All of what we say here concerning Borges' reception and influence is by now received knowledge. It has even become, as we pointed out, an object of study in its own right. It is, indeed, certainly possible to examine it as a phenomenon, to elaborate the reasons why it took place as it did. Of course, the assumption behind these analyses is that we *can* explain Borges' success for finally objective reasons. Once we enumerate the correct factors in sufficient detail, we can definitively know why Borges had the extraordinary impact he did. It is, in the end, to reduce Borges to an effect of his reception. This explanation of Borges' reputation for social and political reasons is the very meaning and consequence of his work. And yet a certain question haunts these analyses, for all of their attempts to relativize or historicize Borges: why Borges? Why was *Borges* chosen for literary canonization and not, say, Alejo Carpentier from Cuba, Julio Cortázar from Argentina or even Marquez from Colombia? Why is it that Borges alone had this overwhelming, transformative effect upon literature and not any of these other socially, historically and perhaps even literarily comparable others? It is at this point that the analyses of Borges' reception look the other way and attempt to identify some immediately recognizable aesthetic quality that would distinguish Borges from his peers. But, of course, the problem now is how to define this quality. It is perhaps by looking at the history of Borges' reception, at the ways he has been taken up and the things people have said in his name, that we might say what makes Borges Borges. To ask this question takes us back, needless to say, to Borges' own exercise in examining the legacy (through those who come 'after' him) of a great writer, 'Kafka and His Precursors'. And the answer with respect to Borges is the same as we saw with Kafka: what all the various successors of Borges have in common is *nothing*. There is no specific thing that looking at Borges' legacy tells us about him, that explains why he was elevated above all others. In a sense, then, cutting across the attempt to account for Borges' reputation in social and historical terms are two paradoxical results. They are the same as those Borges identified with Kafka: Borges is at once only his reception and Borges has nothing to do with his reception.

Borges throughout his career was fascinated by issues of literary posterity, of the historical fate or destiny of particular texts and authors. In terms of Borges' fiction, we might recall 'The Garden of Forking Paths', 'The Immortal' and 'Pierre Menard, Author of the *Quixote*'. But we might think also of 'Averroës' Search', in which a twelfth-century Muslim scholar working on a translation of Aristotle's *Poetics* is baffled by the meaning of 'comedy' and 'tragedy'; 'The Theologians', in which two theologians who have opposed each other throughout life find their respective doctrines mistaken for each other by God when they die; and 'Guayaquil', in which two academics contend for the right to be the first to bring to light the letter in which Simon Bolivár reveals what went on between him and the General with whom he plotted the expulsion of the Spanish from Peru. We might think as well of Borges' extensive series of essays taking up such topics as the translation of literary classics (Homer's *Iliad* and *Odyssey*, *1001 Nights* and Omar Khayyam's *The Rubáiyát*), the various religions and the enduring nature of Shakespeare and the other writers whom Borges held in highest regard (Dante, Kipling, Shaw, Stevenson). It is very easy to read what Borges says here in terms of the ironies and reversals of history, the relativity and impermanence of truth and the misunderstandings and transformations between cultures. But, if we read these texts closely, we will discover *another* logic, at once contradicting and making possible this first one. For what we notice is that the various authors and writings Borges discuses here are not simply caught up in the processes of historical reception and transformation, but seem also to speak of them. The subsequent scene of interpretation, which in some cases can occur centuries after the text was originally written, can appear to be what the text is *about*, what it predicts for itself. If these authors and their texts appear to understand that they are open from the beginning to another, arise only as an effect of their reception, they also somehow take this into account, so that no matter how they are actually interpreted this is what they can already be seen to be speaking of all along. It is this that would be the true 'universality' that allows the relativity and historicity of cultures that is usually understood to be Borges' universality.[13]

What is this finally to say? It is worth paying attention to the uncannily repeated accolade Borges pays to those authors and texts that he thinks are great. It is a compliment that he passes in virtually every case, and that we cannot but think is Borges'

explanation for *why* they are great. We will give only one example of it here, but it is to be found absolutely throughout Borges'
writings. At the end of Borges' short story 'Everything and
Nothing', God says to Shakespeare: 'I too am not I; I dreamed
the world as you, Shakespeare, dreamed your own work, and
among the forms of my dream are you, who like me are many,
yet no one' (*CF*, 320). Borges – for all of his public image as a
genial old man heroically carrying on Western culture from
a faraway place – is proposing something extremely radical here.
It is something absolutely opposed to the classic humanist idea
that great literature is the record of eternal human truths or the
mark of ever-lasting aesthetic worth or even the post-colonial
revenge of the margins against the centre in the name of some
repressed truth. Rather, we might say that for Borges a text lives
on because it both embodies and speaks of that *nothingness that
is universal*.[14] And it is this nothingness that Borges himself, as
we have tried to show at great length, tried to make his subject.
Borges *doubles* literature: he is that void or absence for which
everything stands in, that logic of *everything and nothing* that
allows both tradition and any overturning of that tradition. But
the real 'miracle' of his work – the miracle of fiction, the miracle
his fiction takes up – is that for us this nothing becomes *Borges*.
As God says of Himself and Shakespeare: 'I am not'. Borges,
like that extraordinary series of objects he conjures up in his
fiction, becomes the name for his own absence or impossibility.
We might not be able to define him, he exists only in others'
interpretation of him; but this *is* what Borges is, this is what
Borges takes up in his work and what can be understood only
through it. It is true: Borges *does* only exist within the history of
his reception and interpretation, within the economies of canons
and the expectations of taste. But with the very greatest of
authors, it is also a matter of them preceding all this in making
it possible. We might say that what defines their work is the question of *how* the history of literature comes about. And Borges in
our time and culture has become the name for this thinking, this
thinking of what cannot be thought. This is the destiny of the
very greatest of authors: to live on not as someone but as no one,
to live on not as something but as nothing.

## STUDY QUESTION 1

Trace throughout Borges' fiction and non-fiction the number of times he describes Shakespeare as being everyone and no one or everything and nothing (*CF*, 76, 172, 320; *TL*, 178, 221, 323, 473, 490). Think also about all of those other literary figures and religious and intellectual doctrines described in similar terms in Borges' work. What do all of these people and things have in common? And if it is the fact that they will live on forever, what is this to say about the nature of cultural posterity for Borges?

## CHAPTER 7

# ANNOTATED BIBLIOGRAPHY

'Unceasing human work gave birth to this infinity of books' (*SP*, 393), Borges once wrote in one of his poems. The potential researcher into Borges can certainly feel this when surveying the extraordinary outpouring of books, essays and articles on every conceivable aspect of Borges and his work. I list here but a small fraction of the available literature on Borges. I make no attempt to be inclusive, but merely select what I take to be best examples in each category. It is always possible that I have overlooked otherwise deserving work in a simply unmasterable field of scholarship.

## BIBLIOGRAPHIES OF BORGES

There does not currently exist an up-to-date bibliography of the scholarship on Borges. Such a task can now only be imagined being carried out online. The Borges Center at the University of Pittsburgh has an essential listing of all Borges' own writings categorized by year. The Center also publishes the indispensable, if slightly pedantic, *Variaciones Borges*, a biannual, trilingual (English, Spanish, French) online journal of Borges scholarship. The last bibliography of writings on Borges was David William Foster, *Jorge Luis Borges: An Annotated Primary and Secondary Bibliography*, Garland Publishing, New York, 1984.

## DICTIONARIES OF BORGES

Agheana, Ion Tudro, *A Reasoned Thematic Dictionary of the Prose of Jorge Luis Borges*, Ediciones del Norte, Hanover, 1990.

Balderston, Daniel, *The Literary Universe of Jorge Luis Borges: An Index to References and Allusions to Persons, Titles and Places in His Writing*, Greenwood Press, Santa Barbara, CA, 1986.

Fishburn, Evelyn and Hughes, Psiche, *A Dictionary of Borges*, Duckworth and Company, London, 1989.

## BIOGRAPHIES OF BORGES

Manguel, Alberto, *With Borges*, Thomas Allen Publishers, Toronto, 2004. This book is a superb little memoir, written with great literary distinction.

Monegal, Emir Rodríguez, *Jorge Luis Borges: A Literary Biography*, E.P. Dutton, New York, 1978. This biography reads thinly, is factually flawed and suffers from a simplistic psychoanalytic model, but it does offer irreplaceable first-hand information. Monegal was a friend of Borges, and featured as a character in 'The Other Death' (*CF*, 224).

Williamson, Edwin, *Borges: A Life*, Viking, New York, 2004. Writer David Foster Wallace in a review of Williamson's book for the *New York Times Book Review* is rightly critical of its over-psychologizing of Borges' work and its heavy-handed use of a notion of 'the sword and the dagger' to explain Borges' life. But the book is written with the density of detail and assuredness of fact that we expect from a good biography, and is currently the best available in English.

## STUDIES OF HISTORICAL SIGNIFICANCE

Barrenechea, Ana María, *Borges: The Labyrinth Maker*, New York University Press, New York, 1965. English translation of *La expressión de la irrealidad en la obra de Borges* (1957).

Christ, Ronald, *The Narrow Act: Borges' Art of Allusion*, New York University Press, New York, 1969.

Wheelock, Carter, *The Mythmaker: A Study of Motif and Symbol in the Short Stories of Jorge Luis Borges*, University of Texas Press, Austin, TX, 1969.

These three studies are superb examples of the 'New Criticism', close reading looking for underlying formal structures, applied to Borges.

Blanchot, Maurice, *Le livre à venir*, Gallimard, Paris, 1959. This contains the important essay 'L'infini littéraire: L'Aleph', analyzing Borges' notion of infinity.

De Roux, Dominique, and Milleret, Jean, *L'Herne: Borges*, Editions de l'Herne, Paris, 1964. Includes essays by Jean Wahl, 'Les personnes et l'impersonnel'; Roger Caillois, 'Les thèmes fondamentaux de Jorge Luis Borges'; and Néstor Ibarra, 'Borges et Borges'.

Genette, Gérard, *Palimpsests: Literature in the Second Degree*, University of Nebraska Press, Lincoln, NE, 1997. English translation of *Palimpsestes: La littérature au second degree* (1982).

## BEST OVERALL STUDIES

Alazraki, Jaime, *Critical Essays on Jorge Luis Borges*, G.K. Hall & Co., New York, 1987. This contains John Updike's, 'The Author as Librarian'; John Barth's, 'The Literature of Exhaustion'; and Pierre Machery's 'Borges and the Fictive Narrative'.

Bell-Villada, Gene H., *Borges and His Fiction: A Guide to his Mind and Art*, University of Texas Press, Austin, TX, 2000.

Bloom, Harold (ed.), *Jorges Luis Borges: Modern Critical Views*, Chelsea House, New York, 1986. This contains important essays by Paul de Man, Ronald Christ and John Sturrock.

Molloy, Sylvia, *Signs of Borges*, Duke University Press, Durham, NC, 1994. This is widely, and with good reason, regarded as the best single book on Borges.

Mourey, Jean-Pierre, *Jorge Luis Borges: Verité et universe fictionnels*, Pierre Mardaga, Brussels, 1988.

## BORGES AND LITERATURE

Fishburn, Evelyn, 'Traces of the *Thousand and One Nights* in Borges', *Variaciones Borges* 17 (2004), pp. 143–158.

Irwin, John, *The Mystery to a Solution: Poe, Borges and the Analytic Detective Story*, Johns Hopkins University Press, Baltimore, MD, 1994. This book is very good on the paradoxes of recursion and self-inclusion in Borges' stories and on Borges' indebtedness to detective novels.

## BORGES AND THE QUESTION OF NARRATIVE

Dupuy, Jean-Pierre, 'The Self-Deconstruction of Convention', *Substance* 74 (1994), pp. 86–98.

Kefala, Elena, 'Borges and Narrative Economy: Conservative Formalism or Subversion of Signification?' *Variaciones Borges* 18 (2004), pp. 219–228.

Lafon, Michel, 'Sémiologique de l'espace dans l'oeuvre de Jorge Louis Borges', *Imprévue* 2 (1982), pp. 47–85.

Ramos, Arturo García, 'Jorge Luis Borges: la mímesis de la nada', *Anales de literatura hispanoamericana* 28(1) 1999, pp. 659–680.

All of the above are attempts to elaborate the paradoxical narrative economy of Borges' stories.

## BORGES AND PHILOSOPHY

Alazraki, Jaime, *Borges and the Kabbalah: And Other Essays on His Fiction and Poetry*, Cambridge University Press, Cambridge and New York, 1988.

Bossart, W.H., *Borges and Philosophy: Self, Time and Metaphysics*, Peter Lang, New York, 2003.

Jaén, Didier, *Borges' Esoteric Library: Metaphysics to Metafiction*, University Press of America, Lanham, MD, 1992.

In truth, none of these is so outstanding, but each offers a good overview of Borges' relationship to a number of religious and philosophical doctrines.

## BORGES AND SCIENCE AND MATHEMATICS

Hayles, N. Katherine, *The Cosmic Web: Scientific Field Models and Literary Strategies in the 20th Century*, Cornell University Press, Ithaca, NY, 1984.

Martínez, Guillermo, *Borges y la matemática*, Editorial Universitaria de Buenos Aires, Buenos Aires, 2003.

Merrell, Floyd, *Unthinking Thinking: Jorge Luis Borges, Mathematics and the New Physics*, Purdue University Press, Lafayette, IN, 1990.

These are three of the most fascinating and speculative overall analyses of Borges' work. The Martínez, in particular, for those who have Spanish, is a meticulous and very clear laying-out of the mathematics needed to appreciate Borges' stories.

Amaral, Pedro, 'Borges, Babel y las matemáticas', *Revista Iberoamericana* 37 (1971), pp. 421–428.

Camurati, Mireya, 'Borges, Dunne y la regresíon infinita', *Revista Iberoamericana* 53 (1987), pp. 925–932.

Waldo, Ross, 'Borges y el problema de las series infinitas', *Anales de Literatura Hispanoamericana* 4 (1975), pp. 279–284.

## BORGES AND LATIN AMERICAN LITERATURE

De Castro, Juan E., *The Spaces of Latin American Literature: Tradition, Globalization and Cultural Production*, Palgrave Macmillan, New York, 2008.

Martin, Gerald, *Journeys through the Labyrinth: Latin American Fiction in the Twentieth Century*, Verso, London, 1989.

Zamora, Louis Parkinson, and Faris, Wendy B., (eds), *Magical Realism: Theory, History, Community*, Duke University Press, Durham, NC, 1995.

The Zamora and Faris volume, in particular, is a 'new classic' that deals at considerable length with Borges.

## BORGES AND POST-COLONIALISM

Aizenberg, Edna, *Borges, el tejedor del Aleph y otras ensayos*, Iberoamericana, Madrid, 1997.

Sarlo, Beatriz, *Jorge Luis Borges: A Writer on the Edge*, Verso, London, 1993. English version of *Borges, un escritor en las orillas* (1995).

Sarlo's book effected a 'revolution' in Borges studies with her reading of Borges' stories in the light of contemporary theories of post-colonialism. In fact, in my opinion, these 'realist' readings of Borges often work to *exclude* his most radical dimension.

## BORGES AND TRANSLATION

Cottom, Daniel, *Ravishing Tradition: Cultural Forces and Literary History*, Cornell University Press, Ithaca, NY, 1996.

Kristal, Efraím, *Invisible Work: Borges and Translation*, Vanderbilt University Press, Nashville, TN, 2002.

Waisman, Sergio, *Borges and Translation: The Irreverence of the Periphery*, Bucknell University Press, Lewisburg, PA, 2005.

The chapter on Borges in Cottom's book, 'Conspiring with Tradition: Jorge Luis Borges and the Question of the Miracle', is extremely suggestive, and could be read very closely with Jenckes' idea of the 'messianic' in Borges and Benjamin.

## BORGES AND HISTORY

Balderston, Daniel, *Out of Context: Historical Reference and the Representation of Reality in Borges*, Duke University Press, Durham, NC, 1993.

Jenckes, Kate, *Reading Borges after Benjamin: Allegory, Afterlife and the Writing of History*, SUNY Press, Albany, NY, 2007.

Balderston can occasionally come on like Pierre Menard's 'rectifier' (*CF*, 88), slamming other scholars for the 'appalling' nature of their relatively minor textual mistakes; but, along with Sarlo, he led a revolution in Borges studies in the early 1990s away from the canonical stories of fantasy and towards a more engaged, contextually situated Borges.

## BORGES AND POLITICS

González, José Eduardo, *Borges and the Politics of Form*, Garland Publishing, New York, 1998.

Louis, Annick, *Borges ante el fascismo*, Peter Lang, New York, 2007. Spanish translation of *Borges, face au fascism* (2006).

Monegal, Emir Rodríguez, 'Borges y la politica', *Revista Iberoamericana* 43 (1977), pp. 269–291.

Wheelock, Carter, 'The Committed Side of Borges', *Modern Fiction Studies* 19(3) (Autumn 1973), pp. 373–379.

## STORIES

### 'The Garden of Forking Paths'

Echavarría, Arturo, 'Textual Space and the Art of Chinese Gardening in Borges' "The Garden of Forking Paths"', in Alfredo and Fernando de Toro (eds), *Jorge Luis Borges: Thought and Knowledge in the XXth Century*, Vervuet Verlag, Frankfurt am Main, 1999, pp. 71–106.

Rimmon-Kenan, Shlomith, 'Doubles and Counterparts: Patterns of Interchangeability in Borges' "The Garden of Forking Paths"', *Critical Inquiry* 6(4) (Summer 1980), pp. 639–648.

## 'The Immortal'

Cortes, Daniel F., 'Language and the Unspeakable City of the Immortals', *Signos Universitarios* 18(34) (1998), pp. 123–133.

Evans, Michael, 'Intertextual Labyrinth: "El Immortal" by Borges', *Forum for Modern Language Studies* 20(3) 1984, pp. 275–281.

Pollmann, Leo, 'Con qué fin narra Borges?: Reflexiones acerca de "El Inmortal"', in Karl Alfred Blüher and Alfonso de Toro (eds), *Variaciones interpretative sobre sus procedimentos literarios y bases epistemológicas*, Ibero Americana, Madrid, 1995.

## 'Kafka and His Precursors'

Belitt, Ben, 'The Enigmatic Predicament: Some Parables of Kafka and Borges', *TriQuarterly* 25 (1972), pp. 268–293.

Pellejero, Eduardo, 'J.L. Borges: Los precursores de Kafka. Por una historiografia literaria no historicista', *Philosophica* (Lisbon) 19–20 (2002) (available online under 'Los precursores de Kafka').

## 'Pierre Menard'

Giskin, Howard, 'Borges' Revisioning of Reading in "Pierre Menard"', *Variaciones Borges* 19 (2005), pp. 103–123.

Melis, Antonio, 'Pierre Menard, traductor de Borges', *Vanderbilt e-Journal of Luso-Hispanic Studies* 3 (2006), pp. 131–137.

## 'Library of Babel'

de Behar, Lisa Block, 'The Place of the Library', *Latin American Literary Review* 29(58) (2001), pp. 55–72.

Navas, Ana B. Rodríguez, 'Interpelación y ruptura en "La biblioteca de Babel" y "El Aleph" de Jorge Luis Borges', *Variaciones Borges* 22 (2006), pp. 200–216.

## 'The Zahir'

Dove, Patrick, 'Metaphor and Image in Borges' "El Zahir"', *Romanic Review* 98(2–3) (2007), pp. 169–187.

López-Baralt, Luce, 'Borges, or the Mystique of Silence: What was on the Other Side of the Zahir', in Alfonso de Toro and Fernando de Toro (eds), *Jorge Luis Borges: Thought and*

*Knowledge in the XXth Century*, Vervuet Verlag, Frankfurt am Main, pp. 29–70.

### 'The Aleph'

Merrell, Floyd, 'Between Zero and Infinity', *Journal of Romance Studies* 7(3) (Winter 2007), pp. 87–100.

Rosman, Silvia, 'Politics of the Name: On Borges' "El Aleph"', *Variaciones Borges* 14 (2002), pp. 7–21.

### 'Funes, His Memory'

Johnson, David E., 'Kant's Dog', *Diacritics* 34(1) (2004), pp. 19–39.

Stewart, Jon, 'Borges' Refutation of Nominalism in "Funes el Memorioso"', *Variaciones Borges* 2 (1996), pp. 68–86.

### 'The Lottery in Babylon'

Tournier, Clément, 'La Dimension contre-utopique de "La loteria en Babilonia" de Jorge Luis Borges', in Christian Giudicelli (ed.), *Utopies en Amérique latin*, Sorbonne Nouvelle, Paris, 2004, pp. 145–160.

Van Hee, Victor C., 'A Game with Shifting Mirrors: Non-Meaning and Meanings as Arbitrary Form of Reader Perspective in Borges' *Ficciones*', *Hispanófila* 130 (2000), pp. 53–68.

### 'Tlön, Uqbar, Orbis Tertius'

Fishburn, Evelyn, 'Digging for Hrönir: A Second Reading of "Tlön, Uqbar, Orbis Tertius"', *Variaciones Borges* 25 (2008), pp. 53–67.

Stewart, Jon, 'Borges and Refutation of Idealism: A Study of "Tlön, Uqbar, Orbis Tertius"', *Ideas y Valores* (Colombia) 101 (1996), pp. 64–99.

### LOOK OUT FOR

Eggington, William and Johnson, David E., (eds), *Thinking with Borges*, The Davies Group, Aurora, CO, 2009. This forthcoming collection includes Stephen Gingerich's 'Nothing and Everything: Theoretical and Practical Nihilism in Borges'; Bruno Bosteels' 'Borges as Antiphilosopher'; and Kate Jenckes' 'Borges before the Law'.

# NOTES

## CHAPTER 1

1 Emir Rodríguez Monegal, *Jorge Luis Borges: A Literary Biography*, E.P. Dutton, New York, 1978, p. 358.
2 Mario Vargas Llosa, 'Borges, político', *Letras libres* 1(11) (1 November 1999), p. 24.
3 Cited Edwin Williamson, *Borges: A Life*, Viking, New York, 2004, p. 352.
4 James Woodall, *The Man in the Mirror of the Book: A Life of Jorge Luis Borges*, Hodder & Stoughton, London, 1996, p. 166.
5 Interview in *La Nácion*, 24 November 1974. Cited Williamson, p. 413.

## CHAPTER 2

1 César Fernández Moreno, 'Weary of Labyrinths: An Interview with Jorge Luis Borges', *Encounter* (April, 1969), p. 12.
2 Julio Woscoboinik, *The Secret of Borges: A Psychoanalytic Inquiry into His Work*, University Press of America, Lanham, MD, 1998, pp. 82–84.
3 Ana María Barrenechea, *Borges: The Labyrinth Maker*, New York University Press, 1965, p. 65.
4 Umberto Eco, *Semiotics and the Philosophy of Language*, Indiana University Press, Bloomington, IN, 1986, pp. 80–81.
5 Roberto Alifano, *Twenty-Four Conversations with Borges, 1981–83*, Lascaux Publishers, Housatonic, MA, 1984, p. 24.
6 Borges knew very well the Edgar Allan Poe story 'The Purloined Letter', which is the exemplary instance of this, even writing a preface for it (*TL*, 500). See also John T. Irwin, *The Mystery to a Solution: Poe, Borges and the Analytic Detective Story*, Johns Hopkins University Press, Baltimore, MD, 1994.
7 Ronald Christ, *The Narrow Act: Borges' Art of Allusion*, New York University Press, New York, 1965, pp. 192–227.
8 It would be important here to trace the development of Borges' doctrine of the 'nothingness of personality', from the early essay of that name, in which time means that 'there is no whole self' (*TL*, 8), to the later 'A History of Eternity', in which the stopping of time allows the self to merge into a universality (*TL*, 137–139).
9 We might read Borges' various essays on Zeno's paradoxes of motion ('The Perpetual Race of Achilles and the Tortoise' (*TL*, 43–47), 'The Total Library', (*TL*, 213–216) and 'Avatars of the Tortoise', in Jorge Luis Borges, *Labyrinths*, Penguin, Harmondsworth, 1981, pp. 237–242) and note that it is the same point he is making in all of them: it is only *between two points* that space is infinitely divisible.

## CHAPTER 3

1  Andrew Hurley, 'Blown Away by the Borges Style', *The Independent* (20 January 1999), p. 7.
2  Carlos Fuentes, *La nueva novela hispanicoamericana*, Joaquín Mortiz, Mexico, 1969, p. 26.
3  John Sturrock, *Paper Tigers: The Ideal Fictions of Jorge Luis Borges*, Clarendon Press, Oxford, 1977, pp. 113–122; and Jean-Clet Martin, *Borges: Une biographie de l'éternité*, Éditions de l'éclat, Paris, 2006, p. 11.
4  Harold Bloom, *The Anxiety of Influence: A Theory of Poetry*, Oxford University Press, New York, 1997; and Gérard Genette, 'L'utopie littéraire', in *Figures I*, Éditions du Seuil, Paris, 1966.
5  David Carrier, 'Art without its Artists?', *British Journal of Aesthetics* 22 (1982), pp. 233–244.
6  For a survey of this, see Anthony J. Cascardi, 'Mimesis and Modernism: The Case of Jorge Luis Borges', in Jorge Gracia, Carolyn Korsmeyer and Rodolphe Gasché (eds), *Literary Philosophers: Borges, Calvino, Eco*, Routledge, New York, 2002, pp. 109–128.
7  Jean Ricardou, *Problèmes du nouveau roman*, Éditions du Seuil, 1967; and Gérard Genette, *Palimpsestes: Literature in the Second Degree*, University of Nebraska Press, Lincoln, NE, 1997.
8  Beatriz Sarlo, *Jorge Luis Borges: A Writer on the Edge*, Verso, London, 1993.
9  Daniel Balderston, *Out of Context: Historical Reference and the Representation of Reality in Borges*, Duke University Press, Durham, NC, 1993.
10  Edwin Williamson, *Borges: A Life*, Viking, New York, 2004, pp. 236–238.
11  Georges Charbonnier, *Entretiens avec Jorge Luis Borges*, Gallimard, Paris, 1967, p. 20.
12  See the edited anthology by John O. Stark, *The Literature of Exhaustion: Borges, Nabokov and Barth*, Duke University Press, Durham, NC, 1974.
13  Perla Sassón-Henry, *Borges 2:0: From Text to Virtual World*, Peter Lang Publishing, New York, 2007; and Stefan Herbrechter and Ivan Callus (eds), *Cy-Borges: Memories of the Posthuman in the Work of Jorge Luis Borges*, Bucknell University Press, Lewisburg, PA, 2009.
14  Guillermo Martínez, *Borges y la matemática*, Editorial Universitaria de Buenos Aires, Buenos Aires, 2003; and William Goldbloom Bloch, *The Unimaginable Mathematics of Borges' Library of Babel*, Oxford University Press, Oxford and New York, 2008.

## CHAPTER 4

1  Sturrock, *Paper Tigers*, p. 22.
2  For a survey of Borges' relationship to a number of philosophical doctrines, see W.H. Bossart, *Borges and Philosophy: Self, Time and*

*Metaphysics*, Peter Lang, New York, 2003; for Borges' relationship to the Kabbalah, see Jaime Alazraki, *Borges and the Kabbalah: And Other Essays on His Fiction and Poetry*, Cambridge University Press, Cambridge, 1988; for Borges' relationship to Gnosticism, see Horacio E. Lona, 'Borges, la gnosis y los gnósticos', *Variaciones Borges* 15 (2003), pp. 125–150.

3 Didier T. Jaén, *Borges' Esoteric Library: Metaphysics to Metafiction*, University Press of America, Lanham, MD, 1992.

4 For Borges' relationship to midrash, see Myrna Solotorevsky, 'The Model of Midrash and Borges' Interpretative Tales and Essays', in Geoffrey Hartman and Sanford Budick (eds), *Midrash and Literature*, Yale University Press, New Haven, 1986, pp. 253–264; for Borges' relationship to scepticism, see Donald Shaw, *Ficciones*, Grant and Cutler, London, 1976.

5 Jaime Rest, *El laberinto del universo: Borges y el pensamiento nominalista*, Fausto, Buenos Aires, 1976.

6 See, for example, Jean de Milleret, *Entretiens avec Jorge Luis Borges*, Éditions Pierre Belfond, Paris, 1967, p. 22.

7 Gene H. Bell-Villada, *Borges and His Fiction: A Guide to His Mind and Art*, University of Texas Press, Austin, TX, 2000, pp. 223, 226.

8 Humberto Núñez-Faraco, 'The Theme of Lovesickness in *El Zahir*', *Variaciones Borges* 14 (2002), pp. 115–155.

9 Carter Wheelock, *The Mythmaker: A Study of Motif and Symbol in the Short Stories of Jorge Luis Borges*, University of Texas Press, Austin, TX, 1969.

10 Borges was familiar with the 'aleph' that mathematician Georg Cantor used to designate the cardinality of an infinite set. But more at stake in his stories are the paradoxes of set theory that arose in the wake of Cantor's work. The most important of these was the Russell Paradox, which considers the set of all sets that *don't* contain themselves (*TL*, 250). This set contains itself as a member if it does *not* contain itself as a member, and does not contain itself as a member insofar as it *does* contain itself as a member. The same paradox can be posed by asking: does the barber who shaves all those who do not shave themselves shave himself? We see this paradox in 'The Aleph', but also throughout all of Borges's stories in the way we have tried to make clear here.

11 See also 'From Allegories to Novels', in which Borges points out, against the attempt to oppose allegories and novels, that 'the abstractions [of allegories] are personified; there is something of the novel in every allegory', while 'the individuals that novelists present aspire to be generic; there is an element of allegory in novels' (*TL*, 339–340).

12 Floyd Merrell, *Unthinking Thinking: Jorge Luis Borges, Mathematics and the New Physics*, Purdue University Press, Lafayette, IN, 1990, p. 80.

13 Sylvia Molloy, *Signs of Borges*, Duke University Press, Durham, NC, 1994, p. 74.

14 Borges speaks of this idea of memory always being a memory of memory in Richard Burgin, *Conversations with Jorge Luis Borges*, Holt, Rinehart & Winston, New York, 1969, p. 28.

## CHAPTER 5

1 Patricia Waugh, *Metafiction: The Theory and Practice of Self-Conscious Fiction*, Routledge, London, 2002, p. 3.
2 Maggie Ann Bowers, *Magic(al) Realism*, Routledge, London, 2004, p. 3.
3 David William Foster, 'Borges and Structuralism: Toward an Implied Poetics', *Modern Fiction Studies* 19(3) (Autumn 1973), p. 349.
4 Suzanne Jill Levine, 'The Latin American Novel in English Translation', in Efraín Kristal (ed.), *The Cambridge Companion to the Latin American Novel*, Cambridge University Press, Cambridge and New York, 2005, p. 305.
5 Lisa Block de Behar, *Borges: The Passion of an Endless Quotation*, SUNY Press, Albany, NY, 2003, p. 125; and Sylvia Molloy, *Signs of Borges*, pp. 39, 100, 125.
6 Woodall, *The Man in the Mirror*, p. 120.
7 Bell-Villada, *Borges and His Fiction*, pp. 117–118.
8 Martin Stabb, *Borges Revisited*, Twayne Publishers, Boston, MA, 1990, p. 62.
9 Woodall, *The Man in the Mirror*, p. 117.
10 Jaén, *Borges' Esoteric Library*, p. 194.
11 James E. Irby, 'Borges and the Idea of Utopia', in Lowell Dunham and Ivar Ivask (eds), *The Cardinal Points of Borges,* University of Oklahoma Press, Norman, OK, 1972, p. 44.
12 Sarlo, *Jorge Luis Borges*, p. 70.
13 Donald Shaw, 'Jorge Luis Borges: *Ficciones*', in Philip Swanson (ed.), *Landmarks in Latin American Fiction*, Routledge, London, 1990, p. 35.
14 Jorges Luis Borges, 'Ellery Queen: The New Adventures of Ellery Queen', *Sur* (July 1940), p. 61.
15 Irby, 'Borges and the Idea of Utopia', p. 42.
16 Bossart, *Borges and Philosophy*, p. 32.
17 Bell-Villada, *Borges and His Fiction*, p. 138.
18 See on this recursivity or circularity between Tlön and the world, Merrell, *Unthinking Thinking*, pp. 165–166; and N. Katherine Hayles, *The Cosmic Web: Scientific Field Models and Literary Strategies in the 20th Century*, Cornell University Press, Ithaca, NY, 1984, pp. 145–146.
19 It is intriguing that Umberto Eco does not specifically mention 'Tlön' in his 'Abduction in Uqbar', in *The Limits of Interpretation*, Indiana University Press, Bloomington, IN, 1991. The story would be a perfect instance of the Sherlock Holmes method of solving a crime by remarking on the *absence* of something or on something *not* happening.

## CHAPTER 6

1 Orhan Pamuk, *Other Colours: Essays and a Story*, Faber And Faber, London, 2007, p. 367.

2 Joseph Bottum, 'Aesop Gone to Seed', *Books & Culture: A Christian Review* (November/December 2008), p. 16.

3 Ilan Stevens, 'Rebel Takes His Position in the Canon', *The Australian* (8 April 2009), p. 35.

4 Marcela Valdes, 'Windows into the Night', *The Nation* (13 March 2008), p. 3.

5 Stefan Herbrechter and Ivan Callus, 'Posthumanism in the Work of Jorge Luis Borges', in Claire Taylor and Thea Pitman (eds), *Latin American Cyberculture and Cyberliterature*, Liverpool University Press, Liverpool, 2007, p. 183.

6 David D'Arcy, 'Guillermo de Toro, Ever the Romantic, Never Ironic', *GreenCine* (31 December 2006), pp. 1–3. (Accessed Online).

7 Woodall, *The Man in the Mirror*, p. 261.

8 Kate Jenckes, *Reading Borges after Benjamin: Allegory, Afterlife and the Writing of History*, SUNY Press, Albany, NY, 2007, pp. 108–117.

9 Cited Williamson, *Borges: A Life*, p. 259

10 Cited Martin Stabb, *Jorge Luis Borges*, Twayne Publishers, Boston, MA, 1970, p. 138.

11 Cited Woodall, *The Man in the Mirror*, p. 123.

12 Bell-Villada, *Borges and His Fiction*, pp. 282–283.

13 For an essay taking up Borges' work in terms of this kind of 'universality', see Bruno Bosteels, 'Borges as Antiphilosopher', *Vanderbilt e-Journal of Luso-Hispanic Studies* 3 (2006), pp. 23–31.

14 This would be some way of reading Borges' desire to incorporate all other literatures in an 'immortal' writing, as outlined by Christ in his *The Narrow Act*.

# INDEX OF CONCEPTS

# INDEX OF NAMES

# INDEX OF NAMES